GOD
it's MONDAY

Some Reflections
on the History of
Industrial Mission

DONALD M ROSS

SCOTTISH CHURCHES INDUSTRIAL MISSION

SAINT ANDREW PRESS

First published in 1997 by
SAINT ANDREW PRESS
121 George Street, Edinburgh EH2 4YN

on behalf of
SCOTTISH CHURCHES INDUSTRIAL MISSION

ISBN 0 86153 240 6

British Library Cataloguing in Publication Data
A catalogue record for
this book is available
from the British Library

ISBN 0861532406

The Author acknowledges with gratitude the use of material on pages 60-62 from *The Manpower Services Commission in Scotland* (Edinburgh University Press). Used by permission.

This book has been set in 10/12 pt Times Roman.

Cover design by Mark Blackadder.
Typesetting by Lesley A Taylor.
Printed and **bound** by Athenaeum Press Ltd, Gateshead, Tyne & Wear.

GOD

it's MONDAY

Contents

Preface

DONALD ROSS has a unique qualification for the task of recording the history of Industrial Mission in Scotland. This is a timely record. Thirty years of hands-on experience in this prophetic ministry give him the right to tell its story. It's a story told from the inside by one whose service as an insider has forged links with the leading figures in Industrial Mission in Scotland, in the United Kingdom, and beyond our shores. Indeed Donald's record is a tapestry of friendships made across the varied skein of Scotland's industrial life.

From his pastoral beginnings in Church extension in one of Glasgow's sprawling housing estates, Donald Ross describes his engagement with a host of people within and outwith the Church, always convinced that the Kingdom is not confined by the structures of any institution, even those of the Church. His ministry has been on the margins of the institution, because that is always the place of the true prophet.

The story he tells reveals one of the sustaining motives of all industrial mission since Ted Wickham's pioneering commitment to the melting shops of Sheffield and Horst Symanowski's prophetic work in post-war Germany. Horst Symanowski wrote: 'God himself took man more seriously than the theologians do. Otherwise he wouldn't have walked the earth in the man Jesus.'

Donald's account tells how the seeds these pioneers have sown were able to take root and grow to maturity in Scotland. He always enjoyed the opportunity of commending the Good News of Christ to those who were either opposed to it or would certainly not call themselves Christians. He did this in so many ways: in words, of course; in ecumenical open-ness, because that was his style; in his constant advocacy for those *in extremis* – the unemployed, the alcoholic, the person whose job was at risk. Above all, he commended the Gospel by his unfaltering determination to stand beside working people. Like his Lord, he made the unpopular his friends as cheerfully as he walked with the employers into the board room or with the shop stewards onto the factory floor. That remains the acid test of industrial mission.

In these pages, as in his ministry, Donald Ross passes that test with rare success.

Maxwell Craig
General Secretary
Action of Churches Together in Scotland (ACTS)

PART 1

INDUSTRIAL MISSION in SCOTTISH INDUSTRIAL LIFE

CHAPTER 1

Some Early Experiences

I SET about writing these pages with considerable reluctance. The reason for doing so is because the type of ministry described is one less familiar to many people in the Church. Parish ministry is well known and understood and there have been, over the years, excellent writings illustrating various forms of it. Ministry within the working world is less known and understood, even though the words 'industrial chaplain' have been known for some time. Since a large part of my own ministry has been as an industrial chaplain, there may be some value in recording something of it.

Over the years I have had visitors from different parts of the world who have wished to interview me and others, as they prepared papers and theses about ministries of an unusual kind. Such studies are objective, properly critical, academic, annotated with references and rewarded by the conferring of a degree. What I attempt is none of that. It is subjective in the sense that I am writing about ministry in the world of work as I and my colleagues actually experienced it. We were and are too near to our own ministries to be really objective. We were and are constantly and properly critical, in the sense that we appraised and corrected our efforts in the light of experience.

As in any other sphere of ministry, it changed and evolved in the light of changing circumstances. Since we have been living through periods of massive industrial and economic change, we were constantly stretched, pushed and moulded by events. Yet always, since we were called and ordained into Christian ministry, we were rooted in a Gospel ministry, along with others, in God's working world. To this day I still find it somewhat surprising that I have spent longer in industrial ministry than in parish ministry, which I found so fulfilling and relevant.

In the early years of my second charge there were three ministers in the ministers' fraternal who had each been more than 35 years in their respective parishes. I used to say, with humorous intent and adopting an elderly tremor in my voice, that I would like to be in Fernhill and Cathkin for 'thirty … five … years!' Why not then? Maybe just that a number of strands came together.

Response to the Gospel and the call of Christ in the first place was the result of two strong influences. My parents were both the children of Hebrideans with strong religious roots. Although my father was not a regular church-goer, partly for health reasons, both my parents fulfilled their baptismal vows and ensured us a Christian home and upbringing. We were reared, my sister and I, in the conservative evangelical tradition of Finnieston Church in Glasgow. This was a church much coloured by the strong ministries of Andrew Bonner, D M McIntyre, William Simpson, Alex Fraser, Russell Kennedy and, later, David Orrock. It was a Church with a strong missionary tradition and when I took the centenary service of Finnieston Church, David Orrock told the congregation that I was about the one hundredth minister or missionary produced by Finnieston Church in a hundred years. It was there, during an evangelical campaign, that I made the firm commitment to Christ which has rooted and grounded me since.

Yet there was another profound influence. Donald MacIver and Mary MacAulay, both born in Breasclete in the Isle of Lewis, had eleven children of their marriage, including my mother Margaret and her twin Mary. A life-time of experience, including the loss of infants and the loss of two sons in the First World War, had been nourished and sustained by faith in Christ. They had many grandchildren, but I was fortunate in the most formative years of my life, to be living just around the corner from my grandmother who had survived her husband and indeed a number of her older children. She read the Bible constantly in Gaelic and meditated, prayed and loved. I had daily conversations with her and in the process my faith was formed.

This is not an autobiography, but a tracing of how one minister found himself in the unusual task of ministering in industry. So let me get to that quickly and trace the influence of that part of the Church called the Home Board (now the Board of National Mission).

I was appointed by the Home Board of the Church of Scotland to a student missionary placement on the Island of Tiree, in the Inner Hebrides. Later I was appointed to be student assistant in St Columba's Highland Church in St Vincent Street, Glasgow. This was followed by the appointment to be Licensed Assistant at St David's Knightswood and it was there I was ordained as a probationer by the Presbytery of Glasgow. I was inducted to my first charge at Innerleithen, Craigside in the Presbytery of Peebles in January 1955.

Ministry in the Borders could be difficult and, early on, I noticed that there were many men who never came to Church, although their names appeared on the role. I knew them within the community, so I listed them, recognised the leaders of opinion among them, and went to them individually with my list. I began with those I thought would be the hardest nuts to crack.

I invited them to meet me in the church at 6 pm on a particular Sunday evening. I made sure of gaining the acceptance of the first two or three and made a very obvious large tick against their names on the list. I continued to the others with my visible ticked list. No church elders were invited, but more men came to that event than I had actually invited and there were surprises within the congregation on seeing the return of some of the missing ones. I learned something then about the strategic significance of the workplace and of different methods in ministry.

But again the Home Board. This was a period in Scottish life, in the mid-fifties, when large numbers of the Scottish population were moving from the cities and the old tenements into new towns and into some sixty over-spill areas. The task of the Church was to provide everywhere the ministry of the word and sacrament and the pastoral support of the Scottish people. A massive church extension programme was needed. One church building per month was erected over a 15 year period. It was said that if Boots the Chemists had achieved that, it would have been regarded as a commercial miracle. The need, therefore, was for ministers of around my age to put their energies into such work and I can recall my surprise and trepidation at the receipt of a letter from the Home Board offering me the opportunity to take up any one of five Church Extension appointments then available.

Church extension is not the subject of this writing, but it was immediately evident to me in church extension how much work, a job, its availability, its shift patterns, its security, and its rewards were significant for family life and the life of the community. The local steel, chemical and paper-making industries and the practice of commuting into the city for more distant work, shaped the life and work patterns of the people. Redundancies and unemployment were already present, but for a great many of those employed, shift-working was a key factor. The continental shift system, with 19 different starting and finishing times in any week, was a stress which affected not only those who worked the shifts but the wives and families also. For those men who wanted to worship, opportunities were few. The arranging of three different times of services each Sunday helped, but many found the Church irrelevant.

One experiment I tried with success was to invite men on shifts to a series of meetings on topics related to the effect of shifts on social life, health, family and leisure. I noticed that men appeared at this who would never normally come near the church. The obvious lesson was to try to link ministry to the issues and concerns which people have in their daily lives.

For ministers in Church Extension parishes at that time, working at least twelve or 14 hours a day, all week, the great refreshing event of the year was the annual Church Extension Ministers' Conference convened by the

Home Board of the Church of Scotland. We went there tired and returned renewed from a sense of comradeship with our brother ministers and filled with new ideas and enthusiasm. One such conference proved to be the final trigger propelling me into a new direction of ministry. Cameron Wallace, the industrial chaplain on the lower reaches of the Clyde, was one of the speakers. He pleaded for someone to pick up the industrial chaplaincy task in Glasgow. I went to that conference expecting to continue in the exciting ministry of church extension. I returned with a burden of call which my wife Effie and I struggled with for three months, before deciding that this was a genuine call which we could no longer resist.

During all of this time, and almost synchronous with my own Christian growth and development in ministry, Industrial Mission had had its early beginnings, its phases of experiment, development and expansion. This too was the child of the Home Board and had been blessed and nurtured under God and under the powerful ministries of a great many able and competent servants of God.

CHAPTER 2

Origins
in Scotland

THE current economic scene in Scotland in the last decade of the twentieth century, and the attempt of the Church to relate to it, bears little resemblance to the context in which Industrial Mission began in the early years of the Second World War. At that time the Church of Scotland, through the work of its Home Board, was already attempting to minister to the needs of workers in specific situations. Forestry units from Newfoundland had arrived to undertake urgent work in Speyside, Perthshire and the South, and the Committee reported on the need for an active ministry among them. Church Sisters were appointed as supervisors in the Forestry Units, where girls were employed. They organised their leisure activities and tried to make up for the loss of family life. The Home Board in 1942, as a result of this work, was asked to appoint a Church Sister to act as a chaplain in a factory where a large number of girls were employed.

Work among fisherfolk had started before the War and visitation continued in fishing towns and villages around the coasts. Contact was maintained with girls in their own homes and with the families of men on War service. The Home Board, early in the War, in its reports to the General Assembly of the Church of Scotland, recognised that practically every man and woman not eligible for enlistment in His Majesty's forces, was working long hours, often at very hard work, and often seven days a week. Many who would worship regularly could not do so. 'It is,' said the report, 'the duty of the Church to go to the people if the people are not able to go to the Church .... The Church much seek to serve the spiritual needs of those who work in industry.'

The concern of the Home Board was very much to do with the decline of church-going, diminished interest in religion, loss of members, anti-church feeling and suspicion of organised religion. Though there was in industry a splendid nucleus of faithful Christians, for many the reality of God and the meaning of Christ in the world was missing. It was in its report to the 1942 General Assembly of the Church of Scotland that its Home Board first recognised the need and the opportunity to undertake ministry and mission in industry. If any date therefore could be selected as the formal birth of industrial mission, this was it.

The Home Board reported that one of its members, the Revd William Bodin, had been appointed and set apart to organise the approach of the Church to men and women in industry. This was not a full-time appointment but he was appointed 'to promote and develop the work of relating the Church to industry and to arrange industrial chaplaincies'. He negotiated with companies, persuaded ministers to act as chaplains and built strong links with all kinds of industries and trade union organisations. This opened a period which continued for many years. During that period, the Church of Scotland's General Assembly heard of increasing numbers of chaplains appointed to firms throughout Scotland. By 1946, there were 230 local industrial chaplains and two years later the General Assembly learned that there were 25 industrial concerns 'awaiting the appointment of chaplains'.

In 1942 one minister, Ian Fraser, who had finished his studies at New College, Edinburgh, believed that he was being called to do something about the gap between industry and the Church. He was appointed by the Home Board as an industrial chaplain. He was already a member of the Iona Community and took a job as a labourer in a paper-mill where he was recognised by the Church and the company as a 'labourer-pastor'. This preceded the later worker-priest movement in France or the start of industrial mission in Sheffield, where industrial mission began in England.

Ian Fraser, then and since, pressed the need for the Church no longer to think of industry as a foreign field. He was paid during this experiment by the Home Board. The fact that the stipend for a probationer at that time was the same as a labourer, helped him to identify with the other labourers. This experiment continued for two years, but although it had been a success it was not immediately followed up. Throughout Ian Fraser's later ministries in parishes, Scottish Churches' House and the World Council of Churches, he continued to explore outreach.

George Wilkie was another pioneer. When he finished his studies at New College, he worked for several years at the Canongate in Edinburgh as Organiser of the Young Christian Workers' League. George MacLeod (the founder of the Iona Community) had seen the need for a youth organisation which would assist young people to make sense of life, not only in their leisure time but also in their work. While the organisation was based in Edinburgh, there were branches in other parts of the country including Glasgow, Greenock, Fife and Dumfries. George Wilkie's task was to develop and to expand the organisation.

Towards the end of his appointment George, who was a member of the

Iona Community, discussed with a fellow member, the Revd Harry Whitley, the possibility of working directly within the shipyards of the lower reaches of the Clyde. Harry Whitley was already a part-time chaplain, and he arranged with Sir William Lithgow and the local shop stewards, for George to work as a minister within the industry. After being appointed by the Presbytery of Greenock, he began by meeting people at all levels. Soon he had established regular programmes of meetings and conferences for managers, trade unionists and Christians in industry, to discuss the nature of faith and work. This experiment lasted for some three years and George's own credibility and sincerity made that area a fertile place for later developments in industrial mission.

In 1946 the Home Board reported to the General Assembly its belief that 'the time is not far distant when the Church will require to consider seriously the advisability of setting apart ministers for this work [industrial mission] alone'. By 1947 ministers who had served as chaplains in the forces returned to their parishes and welcomed the concept of 'The Industrial Chaplaincies Scheme', as it was called, as presenting an opportunity to get closer to the life of their people and making for a more effective Christian ministry.

In 1948 the Home Board, having thanked William Bodin for the considerable success he had achieved as part-time Organiser, appointed William MacIntyre as full-time Organiser of industrial chaplaincies. His task was to consolidate the Industrial Chaplaincy Scheme and also to develop the church's work in an additional area, namely with the thousands of men involved in construction work for the hydro-electric industry who were mostly living in work camps. He, with others, drew up a clearer formulation of the aims and methods of industrial chaplains, and published a new quarterly magazine for people in industry called *The Bridgehead.*

In 1953 a new organisation was launched for laymen in industry. A national conference was held under the auspices of the Home Board and 1400 people from all grades and sectors of industry met in the Assembly Hall, Edinburgh. It was unanimously resolved to form the Scottish Christian Industrial Order (SCIO). The intention was to inaugurate branches in congregations and in workplaces. It aimed 'to advance the knowledge and understanding of the Christian faith and its practice; to further the best human relations in industry on the basis of that faith; and to further the application of its principles throughout industrial life and society'.

Quite soon there were 44 church branches. Work-based groups, however, proved more difficult to establish. In spite of the original enthusiasm, the whole venture lasted only a few years. Some believed it would have had a better chance if adequate support staff had been appointed. A further reason was that Christians then, as now, found it very difficult to link faith and work.

To this day there are people who believe the Church lost a good opportunity in not pursuing SCIO. One man especially, Dr Willie Robertson, who acted as the voluntary secretary of SCIO, speaks of those who, like himself, 'clung to the rigging' for a while. He was a professional engineer, one of the instigators of the Scottish Council Development and Industry and later its Director and Executive Vice President. He was also a life-time supporter and helpful critic of industrial mission and, indeed, progenitor of the Society, Religion and Technology Project of the Church of Scotland.

In the early 60s, there was much talk of 'the bulge' of young people leaving school at 15 years of age and making the transition to work. This became a concern for the ecumenical Church and Industry Committee which has oversight of industrial mission in Scotland. It produced a number of publications for apprentices and other young people and for those engaged in industrial training. A further range of publications of this period dealt with *Modern Man and Industrial Relations*, *The Christian in Industry* and *The Church Member and the Trade Unions*.

In 1961 the Home Board agreed to the appointment of a full-time industrial chaplain to work in the shipyards in Port Glasgow and Greenock. The ideal man for the job was Cameron Wallace. He was then minister at Thornlie Church, Wishaw and already a part-time industrial chaplain. He underwent a training course given at that time to industrial executives and then spent long hours with the thousands of men in the immense shipyard industry on the lower reaches of the Clyde. The local presbytery wisely decided to establish a Church and Industry Committee to guide the work: the first such, at presbytery level, in the Church of Scotland.

In October 1962 Willie MacIntyre – after 13 years as Organiser – was inducted to the parish of Tighnabruich. In December George Wilkie, who was now parish minister at St Martin's, Port Glasgow, was appointed to succeed him. Industrial mission, as we have already noted, was in George's blood, having already worked as Organiser of the Christian Workers' League and as a minister in industry, before spending twelve years in the church extension charge of St Martin's.

George quickly devised an appropriate strategy for industrial mission using a selected areas policy. He marked out six industrial areas within which the church should engage in its mission with people at work. Groups, mining courses, conferences for young managers, conferences on over-time and church-based conferences soon developed. During these years there was a steady development from individual pastoral work by chaplains, to the wider work covered by the term 'industrial mission'. Industrial mission was defined as:

*The approach of the whole Church in any area to the industrial com-
munity within the bounds. It is the building of a relationship between
Church and industry through which the truths and insights of the Christian faith may be brought to industry and to the people within it. It is a
two-way process in which the Church by being more aware of the fact of
industrial life may be pressed to discover the richness of its message to
many people in industrial society.*

By 1965 the need for full-time chaplains in others of the key selected
areas – including North Lanarkshire, Dundee, Falkirk/Grangemouth, and
the Glasgow conurbation – was recognised. A year later Sandy Ryrie was
appointed by the Home Board and inducted by the Presbytery of Hamilton as
industrial chaplain in North Lanarkshire with specific reference to the vast steel
industry. He began by working as a labourer for four weeks, going through
the shifts and gaining some personal impressions of working conditions.
Soon he had developed a programme of discussion groups. It was also at
this period that the Churches' Industrial Council was formed. Leading industrialists, trade unionists, academics and others met several times a year to
give guidance to the Church's work in industry. The Council continued with
considerable value and success for some twenty years. In 1967 I was appointed by the Home Board and inducted by the Presbytery of Glasgow as the
full-time Industrial Chaplain in the Glasgow area.

CHAPTER 3

A Minister
is remade

THE work of a parish minister is one thing; the work of an industrial chaplain is something entirely different – but they are in their different ways full and authentic ministries of the church. To move from one to the other was, without doubt, a traumatic experience. From the demanding but familiar task of ministering to a new church extension parish of 12000 people with services, baptisms, weddings, hospital visits, funerals, and a score of church organisations, I shifted to an entirely different set of people, organisations and experiences. A re-orientation of my perspectives and understanding took place quickly in 1967, through the generous and open-hearted acceptance of all kinds of people in Glasgow industrial life. Some of these I vividly recall. All too many of them, however, I can only dimly remember.

Jim Ninmo, a trade union official of the Boiler Makers Society, gave me my first introduction to trade unionism and the history of his own society. He also ensured Effie and me a place on that most moving occasion, the launch of the the 'QE2'. To stand amidst thousands of shipyard workers who had created this immense structure now soaring above us, and watch it gradually move inch by inch down the slipway, was an experience never to be forgotten. I felt then, as I have felt many times since in industrial mission, the realisation of our own small place in the shape of things. Just as each shipyard worker had contributed his own part in the making of this tremendous vessel, each Christian worker, each lay Christian person, each industrial chaplain can only do their own small task in the work of the Kingdom.

Jock Sherriff of the Amalgamated Engineering Union (AEU) offered me friendship and help. I learned from him the motivation of a sincere communist. He took me to the Weaver's Grave at Sighthill and told me of the significance of the struggle for worker's rights. He taught me the industrial relations procedures of the engineering union and took me to visit Mr Armstrong, Director of the Engineering Employers' Association (EEA). He and Jock Sherriff allowed me to sit in on a number of negotiations currently underway.

Before commencing any regular chaplaincy, I was able to visit a number of engineering shops, shipyards and plants. I went round Howdens with a part-time Methodist chaplain, Ted Avary. I visited Stephen's Yard in Govan Road with the manager. I met the Personnel Department at Templeton's Carpets and the training manager at Sir William Arrols. I visited Fairfields and met some of the yard managers and shop stewards. In the Convener's office I met, not only the then Convener, Alex McGuinness, but, sitting at a small side table, a man I would get to know much better, Jim Airlie.

Through the good offices of George Wilkie, the Industrial Organiser, I was able to meet a number of people who gave me a broader perspective of the industrial scene. Alan Gay, then in charge of the School of Management Studies of Strathclyde University based at Chester's College in Milngavie, provided me with a very valuable overview. Jim Haig of the Industrial Training Services introduced me to the changes then taking place in the training world. I met also the regional training officer of the Engineering Industry Training Board.

Fortunately I already knew a number of men employed in companies throughout the area and was able to visit Coates of Paisley with Robert Passway, their chief engineer; United Biscuits with their personnel manager Alastair Littlejohn; and Weirs of Cathcart with Sam Aitkenhead, the much loved local chaplain who also arranged for me to meet the Shop Committee. I met Hugh Wyper of the Trades Council and attended my first meeting of the Trades Council.

Through one or two of my brother ministers I was able to meet some leading businessmen. I thought deeply about the comment of one of them regarding the kirk session of which he was a member, along with many highly professional business managers. He said, 'There we sit, spending two hours over a decision anyone of us would take in two seconds'.

During this early period I was also attempting to educate myself in a number of ways for this new sphere of work. The Industrial Society was a well-known organisation which provided training on a wide variety of subjects, and I benefited from attending a number of these. I also enrolled in a number of courses being held at the University of Glasgow's Extramural Department. One of these was an industrial relations course and this was particularly valuable because it brought me into weekly contact with about twenty other people who were mostly working in personnel departments of companies in the city. At the same time I learned a great deal from a Wednesday evening discussion group which we initiated between six Christians and six Communists. I recall one evening at the Trades Centre in Carlton Place meeting Jimmy Reid, the then Secretary of the Communist Party. During discussion I mentioned that I was not really much of an economist. Jimmy

13

Reid immediately interjected with the words, 'Well you had bloody well better be!' Another very important learning process for me was regular participation with a group of leading trade union officers in Glasgow and a similar number of managers in the Duke of Edinburgh's Study Groups on industry.

Another interesting and valuable friend I met early on was Father Vincent Cowley. He was a Catholic priest, but much in touch with industry in a very different way from me. He said, for instance, that he would not be seen dead on a shop floor. I always argued about his role, which was largely that of ensuring the defeat of communist candidates for trade union posts, but nevertheless through our friendly arguments we learned from each other. Another man met at this initial period who became a close friend and colleague was the Revd Jim Mack. He was Methodist Superintendent of the Partick Methodist Circuit and, although not an industrial chaplain, he had some knowledge of industrial mission in the North East of England. He agreed to meet with me regularly as a personal support to me in my task. Helpful also at the same time was Barry Parker, who had been an industrial chaplain but had now chosen to work as a bus driver, as a kind of worker priest.

Board rooms and director's dining tables were unfamiliar territories to me in those days. George Wilkie knew Olav Thornton, then managing director of Rolls Royce in Hillington, Glasgow, and through his good offices I was invited to visit Rolls Royce. I was privileged to get some impressions of what was then regarded as one of the crown industrial plants in Scotland, with high-specification engineering products for the aero industry. I still recall the feeling of seeing two worlds living on the one site when I was taken, towards lunchtime, from the tour of the industrial plant to what seemed to me to be the sybaritic atmosphere of the directors' rooms and dining table. The six or seven directors I met around this table showed a friendly interest in the concept of industrial chaplaincy. I learned to live in many other companies, as others had to, with the apparent class or rank divide which pervaded most industrial companies of the time.

I had been given a list of ministers who were recognised as part-time industrial chaplains in Glasgow and I was delighted to make contact with them. Warm-hearted Sam Aitkenhead I have already mentioned, and Ted Avary, a Methodist, was a frequent visitor at Howdens. I discovered, however, that a number of the listed chaplaincies were entirely nominal. It was through contacting a Methodist minister who worked with Sternes, an engineering firm in Maryhill, that I got the first opening onto a shop floor. He wished to hand over his chaplaincy and I began visiting the three hundred men there every Wednesday. Here, through contact with shop stewards, managers, foremen, training officers, apprentices and others, I felt myself becoming, for the first time, a fulfilled minister in industry.

By the beginning of December that year, I was visiting Davy United on Thursdays. This was a very large engineering company in Bridgeton with separate plants at Polmadie. In addition, I was regularly visiting and speaking to the apprentices at the Training School at Sir William Arrols.

During these first two or three months, two other events were of importance to me. One was to meet for the first time, my colleagues in industrial mission in a wider context than Glasgow or Scotland. The William Temple College was then located at Rugby and it was there I first met my Church of England opposite numbers, 150 of us doing similar jobs in different parts of the country. It was stimulating and rewarding, a further learning experience. I became aware that not only had we a great deal to learn from our colleagues in England, they had a high regard for the small Scottish Industrial Mission.

Just before I joined Industrial Mission, preparations had already begun for a major conference to be held in Glasgow. The 1968 Baird Hall Conference became a major event in the history and development of industrial mission in Scotland. Some two hundred men and, a mark of those male dominant days in industry and the Church, only four women, gathered at Baird Hall from Friday evening to Sunday afternoon. They represented most levels of employment and came from a wide spectrum of industrial life. They were welcomed by the Lord Provost of Glasgow and the Principal of Glasgow University.

George Wilkie, Cameron Wallace and Sandy Ryrie had already carefully chosen the theme of 'Man in the making of the new industrial society'. The key speakers were Horst Symanowski, the founder of the Gossner Mission in Germany, and Dr Willie Robertson, Chief Executive of the Scottish Council, Development and Industry. Considerable effort went into the preparation for the working parties on such themes as effort and reward, the responsible use of power, change, redundancy and adaptability, the effect of industrial time on human life, responsibility and participation in British Industry, and world need.

Along with one of our key laymen, industrial director Archie McCunn, I had to ensure the effective operation of the group discussing the responsible use of power. I found extremely valuable the various working groups which met at my own home and elsewhere. I still value the amount of reading I did for this to ensure my own comprehension of this vast subject. I was interested to discover later that George Velten of the French Protestant Industrial Mission had translated the paper I wrote for the conference into French. Symanowski's address was memorable and effective. He described the twisting of a bamboo stick. He related this to the pressures many managers and others in industry experienced at the point of stress. Many at the conference identified with that pressure.

It was, however, our own Willie Robertson who made the Baird Hall Conference a landmark. Willie was, and I am glad to say is, a deeply spiritual man, an elder of the Kirk, and one of the most far-seeing industrial thinkers of the Scottish community. He spoke of the massive changes taking place in society through the impact of technology. 'When I wait for the Church to speak on these questions I hear only silence,' he said. He called for the appointment of someone who would assist the Church in its thinking for this new era of change – ' … not a behavioural scientist, not a social scientist, not a theologian, but somebody with science and technology in his bones'. This not only stimulated industrial mission to a fuller commitment to the issues which industrial and technological life threw up for people and society, but led in time to the establishment by the Church of Scotland of the Society, Religion and Technology Project. This was the first such appointment in Europe and is a project which has made a unique contribution to church/world thinking under a succession of most able directors, not least its first, Dr John Frances. Its work is now recognised world wide.

Much of my reflections and discussions with my colleagues revolved around the basic question of how we could, in an effective way, minister the Gospel of Christ to the people, issues and the structures of industry. I recall being interviewed by the journalist, Chris Baur, for a Home Board publication about the task. From what I said he gave it the headline, 'Donald Ross has a new voice'. Until that time, however, I was using my ears more than my voice, having come from a parish ministry with three services, at least, each Sunday, and umpteen meetings in which I was the speaker. I had no pulpit, nor did I desire one in industry. Rather I felt it was important for me to encourage others to reflect on the meaning of what was happening to them. I believed deeply that God was working through people in their ordinary, daily working lives and that it was important for people to discern the activity of God and to follow him on Mondays to Saturdays as well as on Sundays.

One unusual event took place in December of that first year. MacLellan Rubber was a company owned and directed by a family of Christians. I was invited to conduct a service for the workforce. I had considerable doubts about this kind of service, in some sense being imposed upon the employees. One of the directors told me they had been praying frequently for this service, but in spite of my doubts I did take it. Along with the worship, it contained a vote of thanks and gifts to individual employees.

These first four months of industrial mission – September to December 1967 – became for me a crash course in a new form of ministry. The parish ministry is a sphere where the tasks are fairly clear. There is a role expectation. This new ministry could be confusing. There were many uncertainties; there were many directions. So many options. So many people. So many places. Such complicated structures. I spent much time in prayer. At times I was elated and others in an agony of doubt.

I entered each industrial context and started in each section of a shop floor with trepidation. But in the process of meeting people, asking and learning about their jobs, reacting to different personalities, discovering the inter-relationships of people and groups, I found I was engaged in a fulfilling and satisfying ministry. I was in direct contact, on a regular basis, with Glasgow people, mainly men and mainly with no connection with any church. I felt an inner affirmation that, however well I undertook other parts of the job, in making these visits I was doing what I should be doing. Daily involvement with directors, managers, foremen, supervisors, and an immense variety of men and women skilled in their own job and full of perspectives on life and industry, was an education in itself. I still felt I needed, occasionally, to sit back with others and reflect about industrial life and issues in the city.

British Rail contacts enabled me to sit in on a number of BR management courses, each of about three hours duration. To this I added the lectures and meetings of the Chartered Institute of Transport. Attendance at the Trades Council in Glasgow and the annual Trade Union Congress were valuable. Membership of the local Employment Committee, first in Bridgeton and then in Waterloo Street, Glasgow, gave me added perspective. I was a member and finally secretary of the Glasgow branch of the Duke of Edinburgh's Central Study Group on Industry. And, above all, as in everything, there was the brotherhood, the insights, and the sharing of my colleagues both in the full-time team of industrial missioners and the growing group of lay men, women and ministry colleagues who shared a vision and concern for God's work and world in industry.

On occasion I had been invited as guest for lunch to the Glasgow Rotary, which met at the Grosvenor Hotel opposite Glasgow Central Station, and later at Trades House. The membership consisted of some 3300 men representing a most diverse cross-section of Glasgow life. The international Rotarian idea was that each club should consist of one person from each type of industry, sector of commerce, profession or occupation. The Church was already represented by the minister of Glasgow Cathedral, the Provost of St Mary's Episcopal Cathedral and the Territorial Commander of the Salvation Army. I must have been invited as representing a part of the Church's work not yet included.

Rotary's ideal was service to the community, to wider society and to international affairs, but it aimed also to encourage good standards of professional and business life. I decided to accept the invitation to join and for seven years participated in its four main activities, as well as enjoyed the weekly camaraderie. Through its Vocational Committee, of which I became Chairman for a time, I was enabled to conduct a number of different programmes which merged the aims of Rotary with aspects of my own job, to our mutual benefit.

The Size of the Challenge becomes more apparent

When I was appointed in September 1967, I became the fourth member of the full-time team appointed by the Church of Scotland. George Wilkie was Industrial Organiser, Cameron Wallace the industrial chaplain on the lower reaches of the Clyde, and Sandy Ryrie the industrial chaplain in North Lanarkshire. We met each month, most often at Community House in Glasgow, to share our experiences and our insights into this unusual ministry. This was for me, and I believe for the others, a very valuable part of each month. We listened and reflected together on our situation within the shipbuilding community of the lower Clyde. Sandy Ryrie was also deeply involved in the immense steel industry, but I found it difficult to see quite how I could find such a depth in Glasgow. It was helpful to recognise the very different place Glasgow was from either Greenock or Motherwell. The communities of the Lower Reaches and towns of North Lanarkshire were really dominated respectively by shipbuilding and steel-making. To find a place within either of them was to find a place for industrial mission within the community. But the size of Glasgow and the diversity of Glasgow made that impossible. As I grappled with the massive job of attempting to build industrial mission in Glasgow, I discovered immense support in these regular monthly meetings with my three brother industrial missioners.

Inevitably, during the first years of industrial mission activity, I often reflected on the aims and purposes of industrial mission. I knew it was an important and strategic sphere of mission, yet there were many questions. I saw, as my colleagues did that industrial mission must be part of the normal and total mission of the Church in an industrial society. Commerce and industry is a formative area of people's lives and largely shapes society. How people deal with their lives, their problems and their opportunities in the sphere of work affects not only work but all of life. If the Christian Gospel means anything, it must relate to this sphere, a sphere in which chaplains had only a supportive role. The front-line, inevitably, comprises the men and women of Christian faith working at all levels in commerce and industry.

Our aim was to discover, with people in industry, the call of Christ to an appropriate lifestyle for our age and support and encourage those who were striving to incarnate such a lifestyle. In support of that we aimed to challenge the conventional wisdom where this seemed necessary and to push back the boundaries of concern. We aimed to work for a change in structures as well as in the inner attitudes, expectations and motivations of people.

It was important to widen understanding, within the churches, of industrial mission. It was also vital to discover lay men and women who might be invited to participate in the task. For both of those reasons I set out to engage in a series of visits to congregations, kirk sessions, men's groups, youth fellowships, and so on. With a number of kirk sessions I was privileged to have an hour set aside for discussion with the minister and elders before their normal business. It was interesting to observe the changed relationship which took place during the discussion. Most of the elders, shortly after arriving at the session, quickly resumed their working personas. They spoke a language with which their minister was unfamiliar, and in which they were revealing attitudes, views and experiences which did not normally come to the surface in the conduct of normal kirk session business. I recall the startled reaction of one minister when one of his key elders, the industrial relations director of a large company, quite bluntly said, 'Look, I take off my church hat on a Sunday night because I have to become a different animal through the week'.

I recall the meeting of the kirk session of Pollock St James' when Jim Currie, very proudly, introduced a man as a shop steward at Fairfields and one of his elders. Jim's jaw dropped a mile, however, when the man said that when he agreed to become an elder, he decided that he would be a good one, so he gave up being a shop steward.

Jim Maitland invited me to speak at an afternoon conference for his elders at Livingston. That was an interesting event in itself, but it was there I met Norrie MacIntosh, then of the Draughtsmens and Allied Technicians Union and Convener at Burroughs Machines, who remains a supporter of industrial mission and a valuable member of the Churches Industrial Council to this day.

On occasion we arranged lunch meetings with interested ministers to look at aspects of the mission of the Church in sectors of society outwith normal parish activity. Roger Clarke, the minister at Shettleston and part-time chaplain at Gartcosh Steel Works, wrote an excellent article which we published entitled, 'Church and Ministry in the Glasgow Context'. He drew attention to the failure of the Church to be life-centred, rather than church-centred.

When we come to analyse our pattern of church life at the present time, we see how lamentable is the Church's provision of groups specifically designed to help, equip and support our key members in their positions of responsibility in the secular world.

He outlined a number of ways through which the churches could support our laity. Life-centred groups operating in the churches could become a visible embodiment of the Church in the world. Roger developed with success such groups within his own congregation.

The minister of St Francis-in-the-East, Bill Shackleton, had inaugurated in his church at Bridgeton the, at that time, only Scottish branch of an organisation called 'Regnal'. Bill was convinced that this style of men's meeting had a role in the church. I agreed. It aimed to link, for men, the social, physical and spiritual aspects of human life. I recommended one or two men I met in industry and who lived near it, to join. It was picked up here and there in other churches, but I was saddened when it did not really develop.

One of the companies I visited each week was very different from the others. MacLarens Controls in West Street had started out as a small Scottish-owned electronic company, but was now a subsidiary. It was increasingly under the control of a New York based organisation, whose style of management and industrial relations methods were dominating the plant. I saw the signs of stress on the senior managers and later on the foremen and operators. MacLarens produced electronic controls, thermostats and circuits. Ninety per cent of the workforce were women, some of them very young. Their machines were set out in long rows where they did very fine, intricate work. Noise levels were more tolerable than in heavier industry. However, they could talk to each other as they worked and this must have helped them enjoy a day of work which would otherwise have been very repetitive. Pastoral problems with parents, children, boyfriends and husbands soon emerged. In some ways industrial relations were primitive, partly because the women were themselves not keen to become involved in representing the others, and partly because of the remote style of management where power resided in the United States.

One industrial dispute arose from a drink-related problem which set two unions against each other. The Association of Scientific Technical and Managerial Staff (ASTMS) was the foremen's union and they supported a foreman who had ordered a suspension. However the AEU supported those suspended.

Another time I became involved in an unusual way in one particularly disastrous dispute. It was over pay and went on for weeks. Management, who would not speak to the AEU, finally became unobtainable. I took a message from Alex Ferrie, the divisional AEU officer, to the personnel manager who was willing to meet me, but not him, off site. Shortly after, this company, like many others, closed.

CHAPTER 4

Industrial Mission
in Glasgow

T HE base and foundation of industrial mission, as I saw it, had to be
regular works visits. From Tuesday to Friday each week, the morning,
lunchtime and early afternoon of each day was spent in that way. On Tues-
days I visited McLaren Controls in West Street, on Wednesdays Sternes in
Maryhill, Thursdays Davy United in Bridgeton and Polmadie, and Fridays at
Mavor and Coulston and Arrol's Training School. In each plant, in addition to
visiting the shop floor, management and offices, I took classes of apprentices for an hour in the Training Centre. At this stage I invariably wore the
clerical collar, not least because everyone else had an identifiable colour of
boilersuit, overall or jacket. Gradually the element of surprise in people's
reaction to a clerical collar gave way to an easy familiarity. The style of visit
was determined always by the actual layout of the specific plant. At the
beginning I was mainly involved in engineering plants, tool, machine, fitting,
electrical, plumbing, assembly and dispatch shops, which all had similarities
across the companies I visited.

My method was simple. I normally made my presence known to the
personnel manager or another senior manager, as appropriate. Usually I got
some inkling from them of the current preoccupation or industrial situation,
or the state of the orders, or the morale in the plant that day. Thereafter I
would meet the convener of shop stewards or the senior shop steward to get
their perspective. I would then move to the particular part of the plant due for
a visit. I would speak to the foreman or manager and work my way along,
speaking to each individual as he worked. This was normally very feasible.
If a turner was setting a job, I would leave him until he had his machine set
and move on to the next. Generally, in engineering plants, the noise level
allows normal conversation, although at the beginning I did discover that
two or three hours of this left me rather hoarse. I found men invariably open
to speak of their concerns about work, colleagues, bosses, wives and children,
or their outside interests.

Over the years the regularity of such visits gave me the privileged position of knowing many men and I gained from their insights. But, one slightly embarrassing difficulty arose for me, usually at weekends when out shopping with my wife in town. I would meet a man whose face, voice and personality I knew well. I could see him at his machine, but with so many people to know it was extremely difficult to remember the name and even the very plant in which he worked.

Along with Frank Kennedy, a Roman Catholic priest who worked as an industrial chaplain in Glasgow, I became a member of the Friday evening Public Enterprise Group at Strathclyde University It was initiated by Professors Ken Alexander and Tom Carberry. Moreover, the full-time team of chaplains decided to join the Chamber of Commerce where we could learn from the occasional lunch time meetings and lectures.

The normal pattern of work visits included several elements, firstly that of listening to the person or the group in the work situation, and secondly responding to the attitudes expressed. Sometimes I was able to contribute a new insight or perspective in the course of the discussion; sometimes I argued a point if I thought this useful. Frequently I offered pastoral care or human support in a particular situation which was assessed in the light of the Gospel. Many times I felt there would have been value in a more systematic collating of the discussions I had with so many people in so many different contexts. Often we talked about the meaning of life, what people worked for and the meaning of the word 'God'. I now regret not writing up this very fertile field of human feeling and experience. Very few of the people I met were regularly connected with any church, yet most believed in God. Most also prayed at times of stress or emergency. Many had some residual Christian values, a respect for Jesus and often expressed disappointment with the Church. They expected high standards from those who professed a faith and were often disappointed.

I found it necessary, as an aid to remembering people, to draw outline plans of the shop floors I visited. Mavor and Coulston – later to become Anderson Strathclyde – had departments called '17 Spindles', '18 Idlers', '78 Stores', '53 Fitting', 'Maintenance 73', 'Machine Shop 26', 'Tool Room 71', and so on. It was helpful in these situations to mark down the names of people on a drawing of the department.

Though I have many notes of conversations, sadly, with the passage of years, I cannot recall these in too much detail. I remember the man who used to be a shop steward but returned, still in pain, after a heart attack, confessing that he often had to skive in the toilet because of the pain. He told me he had to work on, but he was nervous, because we knew of a man the previous week who had been in pain one morning but died as he left the works.

The works nurse provided me regularly with details of people who had

had accidents or who were in hospital, and these I followed up to the best of my ability. As time went on, one of the interesting discoveries was to meet people in one factory who were related or friendly with people I knew in other companies or on the railway, which I was also visiting. Many men and women felt hemmed in, unsatisfied, or felt as though they were on a treadmill, while at work. Others were philosophical. They found what satisfaction they could in the job and developed many interests outside working hours. It was always a pleasure to meet individuals, many of whom were highly articulate about the meaning of work, about their views of the company or the industrial sector in which they worked. I am certain that industrial companies then, and now, lose a great deal by not tapping into the skills, views and suggestions of their own workforce.

With the Railway Industry around 1972

The image of industrial Glasgow has been shaped by the dominant heavy manufacturing industries of engineering and shipbuilding. It was natural that the early attempts at industrial mission should relate to them. Since Glasgow was also the centre of one of the largest conurbations in the United Kingdom, with hundreds of thousands of people moving across it every day for work, home and leisure activities, it became clear that the fundamental and basic infrastructure of the transport system was, and must be, a key area of concern. I began to explore transport issues, and British Rail in particular, little knowing that it would suck me into itself to the extent that it did. Through British Rail contacts I was able to sit in on a number of private British Rail management courses, on which I gained from the insights of those attending. Each of these courses lasted about three hours. In addition, I was also privileged to attend, as a guest, the monthly meetings of the Chartered Institute of Transport.

Attendance at the Scottish Trade Union Congress (STUC), and at the Glasgow Trades Council, ensured I was in touch with the wider thinking of the trade union movement. Along with Bill Donnolly, a Local District Committee member of the National Union of Railwaymen (NUR), I attended the important British Rail Sectional Council meetings, a key part of the NUR's industrial relations. Membership of the Local Employment Committee at Bridgeton ensured also an understanding of employment affairs in the area. I met the directors of British Rail Scotland, at Buchanan House, and got their general approval to develop local contacts. Maurice Shand, the General Manager of Central Station and related depots, approved the work of industrial mission. I also approached to trade union officials and found them also responsive not least because, by this time, I was an accepted face in the Trades Council and other similar places.

British Rail was a fairly demanding chaplaincy, not least because of the number of establishments which had to be visited. Glasgow Central had over a thousand men (and a very few women) working on shifts in as many as 15 different departments and in five main locations around Glasgow. The mess hall was often the main locus where men came and went all day and night, while providing the passenger and goods traffic necessary for a great city. It had a range of some 18 long tables. By habit and by occupation, and in a type of ranking order, certain tables were reserved for different groups. Drivers had certain tables. Others were for guards, others for Ticket men and so on. I relaxed with them, drank tea with them, and discussed life. The strong religious convictions of the few Moslems often led to interesting discussion from a different starting point, especially in the presence of Scottish drivers and guards, many of whom had little understanding of either the Christian faith or Islam.

Job satisfaction was not high. The essential pride of being a railwayman was eroding. The railway was often thought of as an industry within industry, which everyone needed but did not highly regard. 'If the Station Manager came in that door offering us redundancy money he would be killed in the rush,' they said. Depots at Larkfield, Smithylye, Bellahouston and Polmadie were integral to the Central Station railway system. Permanent way staff, engineering and electrical staff covering every inch of the technical system were also essential. Control rooms, running foremen, supervisors, managers and clerical staff all had their tasks to do, and I was privileged for many years to be, in some sense, one of them.

As in other places I received regular information through formal, and often more importantly, through informal channels. In each place also, the supervisors and the Local District Committee representatives (railway shop stewards) kept me informed about morale and industrial situations. Frequently there were sensitive industrial relations situations, particularly at Larkfield which was regarded as difficult for successive Glasgow Central Managers. There a set of industrial relations agreements going back thirty years was still in place.

One extremely valuable period for me was when I worked shifts alongside different grades of railway staff. I experienced each of the four categories of carriage cleaning and shared the frustration that the 23 cleaners (men because of the odd shift hours) experienced over the stupidities of others in the railway. Adhesive glues, for example, were used to fix small adverts onto glass. They were very difficult to remove. Passengers were often careless disposing of chewing gum which was also difficult to remove.

I also enjoyed the satisfaction of operating, under supervision, the largest destination board in Britain in the great oval shaped window space of Glasgow Central station. This was a meticulous and demanding job for the skilled staff there, constantly under pressure of emergency changes. The movement of goods and passengers through Glasgow Central station was always a constant amazement to me; as was the recognition that, with over 100,000 people every day passing through the concourse, it was the busiest station in Britain.

One of the interests of the job of industrial mission for me at that period, was the sharp contrast between two very different types of industry: engineering and shipbuilding, where the products were very visible; and the railway. Although trains, track and signals were produced by engineering companies, the railway was essentially a service industry engaged in conveying people and goods safely, comfortably and on time. Someone travelling to work or to a social engagement is hardly likely to understand the immense complexity behind the simple journey or the frustrations of achieving it. Quite frequently I would come out of the manager's office at Glasgow Central and notice a small queue of irate passengers ready to make complaints. I would walk twenty or thirty yards along the corridor into the offices of the running foremen for drivers! At Glasgow Central there were 96 guards on a shift. On one particular day 42 were not available for duty for one reason or another, 15 were off sick, and 15 were having their rest day. The fact that they could be off two days on full pay without a doctor's certificate after 20 years service, certainly accounted for some of this problem.

At this time managers were constantly anxious as a result of the re-organisation of British Rail. There had been several major attempts to reorganise, each lasting several years and causing many uncertainties. It was a most unhappy situation for many people. Some knew they might be promoted during the next move; others knew they might very well find themselves in a much less favourable position. One basic problem for men in the railway was that many of them had no skills applicable elsewhere. They felt management had them in the palm of its hand and that they had no option but to stay where they were or to go where they were placed.

In the mid 1970s I was heavily committed – perhaps too heavily committed – to Transport 2000, a group looking at the future for transport in the west of Scotland. The three Scottish full-time trade union officials attached to the Railway Industry – John Walker of Amalgamated Society of Locomotive Engineers and Firemen (ASLEF), John McKelvie of the NUR, and George Dunnipace of the Transport Salaried Staffs' Association (TSSA) – moved at the Transport 2000 committee to have me appointed as chairman, which I was for a number of years. This, in some ways, tied in naturally with my British Rail chaplaincy, and it was from that base that I became involved with transport questions. I had to attend many meetings of the Public Transport Action Committee, the New Glasgow Society, and meetings convened by Transport 2000 itself, not only in Glasgow but in Perth, Inverness and elsewhere. Transport 2000's purpose was to campaign for a more integrated use of public transport facilities, better forms of transport, increased road space, sensitivity to the environment, and the economic benefits of transferring bulk goods and truck traffic onto rail. I became an active member of the Scottish Association for Public Transport (SAPT). Transport 2000 was a UK body, while SAPT was a Scottish one. For a while, the same busy people were trying to give attention to both organisations. It seemed wise, therefore, to merge the two organisations in Scotland. SAPT continues to this day as the leading Scottish public transport pressure group, still affiliated to Transport 2000 and the Environmental Transport Association.

I felt that the work within Transport 2000 was a natural adjunct to my work as an industrial chaplain. There were moral questions about our use of transport and, both at global and national level, the dominance of the private car was a major factor. The cost in human life, the effect on the environment, the misuse of resources, were all factors which society was ignoring. As someone said, 'we have discovered the enemy. He is *us*'. Inside our cars we are each individually a cause of the problem. Outside them we become one of the sufferers. It seemed reasonable then, and still is now, for us to be working towards a better, reliable and more comfortable public transport system within and between cities.

Joint Chaplaincy at Govan Shipbuilders

The formal initiation of Father Frank Kennedy and myself as joint chaplains to Govan Shipbuilders was a very interesting development. We had proposed such a joint chaplaincy, with the support of the then Catholic bishop Tom Winning and George Wilkie, to the managing director of Govan Shipbuilders, Archie Gilchrist, and the shop stewards. One of its opening paragraphs said:

> *Given the Catholic/Protestant situation in Glasgow and the West of Scotland, and the special historic place of shipbuilding in the area, there would be special value in the appointment together as industrial chaplains of a Roman Catholic Priest and a Protestant minister. The Revd Frank Kennedy will mainly develop contacts and knowledge of the Scotstoun division and Donald Ross of the Govan division. The aim will*

be to provide pastoral care and witness to the Gospel for men and women in industry; to assess in the interests of the Gospel, the nature of the influence which the industry exerts both on individuals and on society; and to promote the desire for just-relationships and understanding at all levels in our industrial society.

Frank and I became close colleagues. The men at the yard saw us as part of the same team. We both had to wear the same green hard hats, but Frank frequently raised a laugh by his blatant wearing of a blue rather than a green jersey. The Govan yard of this period employed some four thousand men and was part of Upper Clyde Shipbuilders. Frank Kennedy visited Connels yard in Scotstoun with a slightly smaller workforce. We decided that together we would maintain contact at Linthouse which had about a thousand men. Archie Gilchrist, the Chief Executive, was very helpful, as were people like Ian Farningham in Industrial Relations. They provided us with charts of the production organisation structure, the structure of the industrial relations department, and the names of all the directors, managers, and various heads of departments. Bill Donnelly and Tom O'Neill of the Personnel Department were also very helpful.

The place was an immense area of yards and berths. The appalling noise from the caulkers made me wonder how men could do such a job and remain sane. The stoor, grit, sparks and smoke of blacksmiths shops, welding shops, burning sheds, and plumbing shops, which had been the background for the working lives of thousands of men in Clydeside for generations, became for me quite quickly a familiar sphere of ministry. Though strange, daunting and overwhelming at first, I found myself relaxing in the context of Glasgow working men. There were indeed also some women whose openness, frankness and humour made ministry a pleasure.

Industrial relations is always a key factor in shipbuilding. There were occasional short-tempered walkouts which were due to avoidable smoke, noise or heat. There were classic demarcations with deep, historical roots between unions and even within unions. On the whole, partly due to the experience and practical wisdom of a good shop committee, industrial relations in Govan steadily improved and was streets ahead of neighbouring yards in the lower reaches of the Clyde.

In the very early days of the 'Industrial Chaplaincy Scheme' – in the 40s and 50s – chaplains shared in the training of apprentices. These were the days when apprenticeship was the normal way of working towards a reasonably secure working future. The journeyman tradesman, father figure, mentor, model of the older skilled man, was familiar to thousands of young men in all kinds of trades. Large companies, however, began to systematise and develop more standardised training to widely accepted levels of competence, which were linked to the attainment of external qualifications, such as those of the City and Guilds. The first training schools in which theoretical and practical training was carried out became a natural place towards which chaplains also gravitated. Many chaplains used the opportunity well, though it must be said that there were a few unfortunate situations of men attempting their own brand of theological indoctrination.

Nationally the fruits of the Industrial Training Council, which developed the concept of all-round training for young people in industry, then emerged. Around 35 Industrial Training Boards (ITBs), one for each sector, were established: for example, the Engineering Industry Training Board, and the Shipbuilding Industry Training Board. All of them sought to develop three strands of interrelated training, theoretical, practical and social skills. Within the latter, wise chaplains could participate. This was often encouraged and appreciated by training officers and staff. This field could easily have sucked us in completely, in almost any industry. Steel, engineering and shipbuilding had thousands of young men and a few girls in training who would become the future skilled workforce. It might have been a very wise strategy for industrial mission to place a considerable emphasis on this kind of work, with an eye to the future.

Like many others I was distressed at the abrupt replacement of Archie Gilchrist, the managing director at Govan. His experience has unfortunately been replicated in that of many senior men since. He had loyally fought for Govan, but perhaps more strongly than was in his own personal career interest. The mode of his sacking was brutal. Travelling down by plane for a routine meeting in London, he was unaware that his replacement, Erik Mckay, was already on a plane preparing to take over his post. I have a letter from Archie dated Boxing Day Christmas 1979, thanking me for a letter to him, in which he repeated his respect for the efforts of Frank Kennedy and myself over the years, and a further letter on his departure to a new post in Singapore. He was, and is, a gracious man, but the incident revealed the callous way in which industry can sometimes operate.

George Wilkie's Influence

Without doubt the key figure in industrial mission during my time was George Wilkie. In one way or another he gave his considerable abilities, deep commitment and gracious way of working for most of his ministry, to the growth and development of industrial mission in Scotland. His wise leadership, especially during the 17 years when he was Industrial Organiser, made a place for it that it would never otherwise have achieved. All of us in industrial mission, and in the wider Church, owe him an immense debt of gratitude. I had hoped, when I was a chaplain in Glasgow, that George would continue as Organiser. My own sense of ministry, I believed, was calling me back to the parish ministry which I had always loved. When, however, George left industrial mission in order to become parish minister at Kirkcaldy Viewforth, it seemed appropriate to him, to the Team, and to the National Church and Industry Committee, that I should follow him as Organiser. This was for me the key turning point which would shape and determine my thoughts and actions for the rest of my working life. Now there would be no return to what I knew would be the difficult task of parish ministry somewhere, nor to the peripatetic ministry of industrial chaplaincy in Glasgow. A new and wider responsibility was being thrust upon me.

Already my colleagues and I were discerning major changes in the industrial scene in Scotland and these would demand all the abilities and energies of Scottish Churches Industrial Mission (SCIM), as we now called industrial mission, and in that I recognised I would have an organisational, co-ordinating and even a leading role for which I had to commit myself. In my diary of the period I wrote a simple biblical prayer which I used then and have often used since. I asked that 'I be filled with the knowledge of His will and with all wisdom and spiritual understanding'.

CHAPTER 5

Part of a Wider Missionary Scene

The Rise of the Industrial Mission Association

A S in Scotland, industrial mission began in England as a result of the initiative of a number of individuals gaining entry to industry at roughly the same time. This took place both within the various dioceses of the Church of England and also within the Methodist church in England. It gradually led, in larger urban areas, to the creation of small teams of chaplains. There was a pioneering spirit around and a recognition that this was an essential field of mission, not least because the experience of many Anglican clergy was of the inadequacy of the Church of England parish structure to touch, in any effective way, the lives of many working people.

One of the undoubted pioneers in the field was Ted Wickham, whose study on *Church and People in an Industrial City* became a seminal document. It had a profound influence on the development of industrial mission. He wrote of the necessity of the church learning to 'influence the influencers' within industrial life and structures.

Out of these early post-War beginnings an Industrial Mission Association (IMA) was initiated at the William Temple College in Rugby in the late 1960s. There were many discussions as to who should become participants within it. Would it only be industrial missioners or would it be open to a wider membership? Although it was made for a wider membership, it has been predominately an association of active practising industrial missioners, mainly full-time. There were ecumenical industrial mission teams, usually of between six and a dozen members, in most of the main urban centres in England, with smaller teams in Wales. The Scottish team at that time had four full-time members, and about a hundred part-time chaplains. Teams formed themselves into Regions, usually a grouping in England of several teams, and the Regions elected office bearers to the Central Co-ordinating Committee (CCC) of the IMA which met several times a year in London.

One of the early IMA conferences was held at High Lea in Hertfordshire.

It was attended by Archbishop Ramsay, the Archbishop of Canterbury, and I remember in one group being pressed to ask him, as I did, why the Church of England did not appoint a body similar to the Church of Scotland's Society Religion and Technology Project. I was amazed at his response, which was really to question why the Church should make such an appointment. It was also at this conference that the Archbishop of Canterbury used a phrase very appropriate for industrial mission – that of 'inductive theology'.

While the membership of the IMA met only once every two years, for a week, a system of networks soon developed. Chaplains in different parts of the country whose work involved them in a particular industrial sector – such as coal, steel or shipbuilding, or large companies such as ICI, or who wished to reflect on key issues of unemployment, defence, or women's work – formed a network. By this means they were able to work more effectively, both at the local and national level. They could more easily meet with the appropriate people involved when directing and deciding matters with which the network was concerned. These networks have been useful, but British Industrial Mission would have become much more effective had there been, south of the Border, a national organiser or co-ordinator as in Scotland. Many sporadic attempts have failed to produce a British Industrial Mission Co-ordinator.

The Church's Consortium on Industrial Mission (CCIM)

Industrial Mission, by shear necessity, has to be ecumenical. Some 35 years ago the British Council of Churches initiated the CCIM. This body was made up of the person responsible for the work of industrial mission in the participating churches in Scotland, England and Wales. They were largely people who were not themselves industrial missioners, although one or two were. The CCIM included the general secretaries of the Methodist and Baptist churches, the Director of the Luton Industrial College for the Methodist church, the Catholic bishop who chaired the World of Work Section of the English Catholic Bishops' Conference, an Anglican bishop from the Board of Social Responsibility of the Church of England, a representative from the Welsh churches, and me. I represented the Scottish churches participating in industrial mission. The main task of the CCIM was to guide and support the work of the churches in relation to industry. The chairmanship rotated around the participating churches and I began to chair it for the two year period – 1988 to 1990.

Under George Wilkie, my predecessor, one person was appointed the Scottish representative to both the CCIM and the CCC of the IMA. As

Secretary of the National Church and Industry Committee in Scotland, he represented the Church of Scotland on the Consortium. To save time and travel costs he also represented Scottish industrial mission on the CCC, since it always met on the previous day. After George, I continued this arrangement. This meant that George and I had long continuity on these committees. I saw representatives from the English teams come and go, while I seemed to go forever.

The CCIM has been of value in representing the interests of industrial mission to the main churches and also in producing helpful guidelines for industrial mission, such as on the appointment of chaplains. For two years I was chairman of the CCIM. It was a memorable time, not least because on one occasion I had to write from the Consortium giving an English bishop a row for dismissing a chaplain without consultation. The period of my chairmanship coincided with the development of the new ecumenical instruments, as they were called, covering Britain and Northern Ireland. These marked the change from the British Council of Churches (BCC) to the new Council of Churches of Britain and Ireland (CCBI).

Since the big change, ecumenically, from the days of the BCC was to be the participation of the Roman Catholic Church, and since the CCIM already included Catholics, the Consortium was already an appropriate body. Our English neighbours loved to talk about ecclesiastical structures and we had a rather fruitless two or three years of discussion papers dealing with the change before the CCIM was reformed as the Churches' Co-ordinating Group for Mission to Industry and the Economy.

Industrial Mission Abroad

Those of us working in industrial mission in Scotland were frequently helped by our contact with others doing the same kind of work in other countries. The motivation and sense of mission were similar across international boundaries. Because of social, political, industrial or structural reasons, industrial mission took a different form in each country. Mission has to relate to the actual scene that it encounters.

In France, for instance, there were two main strands. The Catholic 'Mission De France' worked through the worker priest movement. These priests took jobs in French industry and worked alongside others, encouraging them to express their Christian faith through participation in the trade union movement. They also encouraged them to act in solidarity with others, towards the creation of an industrial society shaped by Christian vision. The worker priest movement had been through a turbulent history, falling out of favour with the Roman hierarchies for becoming too closely linked to what the Church saw as communist and atheistic tendencies. Nevertheless it continued.

The other strand was Mission Populaire, the French Protestant Industrial Mission (FPIM). It operated in a very different way from the work in Britain and had much to commend it. Just two or three years after I began in industrial mission, I was one of a group of 21 industrial missioners who went over to visit the FPIM centre in Rouen. We learned about the work of Fraternities, had heated discussions in French and English about the comparative situations we faced, visited the Rouen Port Authority, discussed industrial relations, and, in the evenings, formed a discussion panel of which I was a member, answering questions posed by the French. The FPIM has roots in the Congregational Church in the United Kingdom through its founder, the Revd R W McCall. It operates throughout industrial France and works through a series of Fraternity groups. Each Fraternity is a base of Christian support for people already committed to work as Christians in other organisations such as trade unions, the Blue Cross or community groupings. One of their leaders, Georges Velten came every year to visit us in Scotland and it was our practice for a number of years to arrange meetings of trade unionists, managers and others to exchange views and find mutual support.

Madras industrial missioners, whose task, in a very different culture, was undertaken in a similar way to ours, visited Scotland on a number of occasions. In India they entered factories, held discussions on issues, and sought to support best human conditions. I liked the title of their Mission, 'Christian Service to Industrial Society'. The Christian community in Madras was small and yet the aptly named 'Christian Service to Industrial Society of Madras' was influential in contributing to Madras' industry and society. One of their leaders, Felix Sugirtaraj, stayed with us in Glasgow; and after him, a number of other visitors from Madras came.

In Germany much of the activity of industrial mission centred on lay academies, such as the well-known Gossner Mission founded by Horst Symanowski. They took managers and trade unionists out of their industrial contexts for a period, to study together the development of Christian witness within industry. (The German pastor in Glasgow, Herbert Gunneberg, who had been deeply influenced by the Gossner Mission was very supportive of our work in Glasgow.)

In South East Asia, Korea, Japan and elsewhere, there have been courageous attempts by individual industrial chaplains to fight for workers' rights, at considerable risk to themselves. In the United States, industrial mission developed to some extent, as a result of the influence of English industrial mission. Quite rapidly, however, industrial mission was largely overtaken by civil rights activities.

In Australia and New Zealand, chaplains are paid directly by industry. We have always felt uncomfortable with this. To some extent it arose as a result of a less developed personnel management function in those countries. We felt it made chaplains less free to make an independent Christian critique of industry. Regardless of this, we have been fortunate to meet many of our New Zealand and Australian colleagues.

CHAPTER 6

Doing
Industrial Mission

The Chaplain as Listener

AS a parish minister I had kept a record of visits, noting the family situation and any special or pastoral features. In the very different job of meeting people in a large variety of industrial situations, I attempted to do the same. At the end of each day I recalled the people I had met. I must have filled many notebooks. As time elapsed, and in the aftermath of industrial closures and redundancies, many of those records are long gone. Had I carefully retained them, I suppose these pages could now have been filled with a huge variety of human interest stories and with perspectives on human life from a very interesting cross section of Glasgow men and women.

Conversations often began with the worker's attitude to the work situation. It was always interesting to hear how individuals either echoed the general view of the shop floor or presented their own thoughtful insight. This often led on to a wider discussion about personal attitudes, the individual's view of work itself, its repetitive nature or its interest. So many talked rather helplessly of being in a rut, and of being manipulated by someone else at the top. Many undoubtedly felt they had missed opportunities in the earlier part of their life, and expressed the futility of doing the same thing for many long years ahead in the same or similar little corner of a machine shop or shed.

Conversations often became both philosophical and theological: on the nature and value of work, about guilt, meaning, the human contribution to society, and our interdependence with each other. Don't tell me that in the average Scot there is not still a deep well of intelligent thoughtfulness about all that life presents! On matters of the Christian faith itself there were many conversations with Catholics and Protestants, and with people of no faith at all. All too often I came across people who had received a Christian upbringing but had clearly decided to leave the Church, or had simply drifted away because they felt it no longer important to them. Some spoke with bitterness about the Church. I often became the recipient of real anger over incidents, church members, or ministers, who had aroused in them negative attitudes towards the Church. Those with such views were quick to point out the failings of others in the company who were known to take a leading part in the Church. 'Look at him. He's supposed to be a Christian, and .... !' At times conversations were highly charged emotionally: for example in the aftermath of suddenly announced decisions about redundancies or closures. To be told at the back of eight on a Monday morning that an individual would be working elsewhere in the firm, or not at all, was obviously a shock.

Because I moved between different companies I was often surprised at how awareness of trends in industry and perspectives on life could be so different between companies and unions in the same industry. In one company all the talk would be about the merger of two unions; while, in another, absolute surprise that such a thing should even be considered. And of course there was inevitably football ... inevitably Orange and Green ... inevitably them and us – whoever them and us are – and inevitably sex. I suppose I and my supposedly douce industrial mission colleagues everywhere have seen every variety of pin-up that has been tacked on a bothy, hut, office or machine shop wall. Nevertheless, the substance of the thousands of conversations we have had in industry is not, I am certain, much different from those elsewhere, unless in the rarefied regions of a church not in touch with its people.

Getting to know Shop Stewards

One group of men I particularly came to respect were shop stewards. For some reason, people outside industry often have a negative attitude towards shop stewards. Many take on the responsibility reluctantly, and for a period simply as something they feel they must do to share the load equally with others who will take their turn. Fortunately there are others who are committed to representing their workmates over a period of years. For a few it is a quasi career. Others are motivated by ideology. Some seek personal prestige. Human motivation is always complicated. They are still essential and are regarded so by most wise managers and directors of the companies in which they serve.

Trust is a crucial element in all human relationships. Both management and shop stewards knew very well that I was speaking to them both, equally. I was well aware that I could have been suspected by either group of being some kind of tale carrier. I recall one very angry manager complaining bitterly to me because he thought I had divulged something. His trust improved when he discovered that I had not. Similarly shop stewards were wary at the beginning. Several were openly hostile because of preconceived notions of the Church being more aligned with bosses. The strange truth was that those with the greatest initial hostility, while not accepting the Christian faith, became both warm friends and highly sympathetic to the aims of industrial mission.

Men who were of considerable importance to me were members of a number of clerical unions. The majority of them were members of Burnside church, a neighbouring congregation to my own former parish of Fernhill and Cathkin, near Glasgow. I appreciated their recognition of my need for assistance and we found great value in regular interchanges and discussion. These men continued for many years in support of Industrial Mission, not least Dick Phillips, Bill Bodie and Geoff Fielding.

Contacts with shop stewards in the different companies and industries with which I worked were further enriched by the development of wider relationships within the trade union movement. Trade union full time officials were extremely helpful. My attendance on Wednesday evenings at the Glasgow Trades Council taught me a lot. In some ways it reminded me of the Presbytery of Glasgow, transferred into a smoke-filled room in Clyde Street. The three hundred or so branch representatives discussed with vigour trade reports, industrial situations and the human needs of a changing Glasgow. Fervour and commitment, alliances, voting, reports from committees, all had their echo in the similar body, the Presbytery of Glasgow. I was much helped by successive secretaries of the Glasgow Trades Council – Hugh Wyper, John Reidford and later Jane MacKay.

Few women took on the role of shop steward. One I knew in engineering went to her trade union conference and took a wrong turning during a hotel fire. Her death deeply affected us all. I recall also how devastating it was to be with the family and friends of a young shop steward who had been electrocuted. I remember visiting the family and looking at his body. There was not a mark on it. Stewards in many ways give time and life to help others. One of the few committed Christians I knew, who was also a very able steward, used to tell me how negative were the attitudes in the Church towards him. 'Yet we are taught in the Church to be stewards in the cause of Christ. Why can't they see I am doing the same job for others in here!', he once said.

One valuable learning process, both for me and for the shop stewards who participated, was the BBC broadcast over a six week period of a training course for them. I was delighted when the stewards in one big engineering company invited me to participate in the discussion after the programme was broadcast. Management were not allowed into the room! Around the same time we published a small industrial mission leaflet called *The Role of the Shop Steward.* It began with an identikit picture and citation, referring to the same hypothetical human being from two different perspectives. It is worth quoting.

IDENTIKIT-PICTURE

SHOP STEWARD

Wanted for industrial sabotage, agitator, inciter of strikes, disloyal member of the industrial community; restrictive practiser, restrainer of trade, irresponsible, obstructive, stubborn and crafty, politically suspect, overpowerful – believed to be dangerously active on every shop floor.

Anyone recognising this character should send details at once to the nearest newspaper, which would be pleased to print further evidence of his misdeeds.

CITATION

Shop stewards' medal for ....
To S. Steward for long, gallant and distinguished conduct service in me face of the enemy employer. S. Steward has carried out his duties to his members under dangerous conditions, especially the threat of sack, in exemplary manner. He has overcome difficulties and obstructions put in his path by both employers and union officials. He has sacrificed his own earnings to protect the wages and conditions of his fellow workers. He has been unsparing in the time given to problem-solving, even at the expense of his family and social life. He has suffered malicious attacks from a hostile press, who have failed to understand the voluntary service he gives and his important function in democratic industrial society.

The Mission is extended to Young Workers

As far back as 1969 the churches were finding it difficult to hold young people in their late teens. Church organisations like the Boys Brigade and the Scouts did have contact with boys and girls up to the age of 14 or 15, but

Bible classes and youth fellowships often had to struggle to retain numbers. There were some large youth fellowships and Bible classes in a number of congregations, but these were largely in the more suburban areas of the city. I found very few 16-20 year olds in industry who had any strong attachment to the Church.

Long before my time a number of part-time chaplains had established links with engineering companies and had taken part in training programmes for young people. Each of the companies I visited had a training department giving apprentices an off-the-job first year's training. In the training schools I was invited to take the apprentices for at least an hour each week. I had no intention of lecturing to them or sermonising, but there were plenty of issues which the boys were happy to discuss. Other industrial chaplains had similar opportunities and so we compiled a set of notes for such opportunities. These became a useful tool.

I recall, with some satisfaction, a day of mutual training which was arranged in the training centre at Sternes. I learned all I could about engineering from the training officers and the boys, who spent time instructing me and answering questions. In the latter part of the day we listed the things they wanted to talk about in the weeks ahead. These included war, Biafra, black magic, trade unions, sex, the space age, violence, housing, politics, and scooters.

I did similar work with Sir William Arrol's apprentices on a Tuesday, at Davy United on a Thursday, and at Mavor and Coulston on a Friday. Each of those companies was much smaller than the enormous shipbuilding industry in Glasgow, which at that time had a most effective training department with a regular intake of some three hundred apprentices. Frank Kennedy and I hardly knew how to cope with the immense opportunity open to us of regularly working with these lads. We worked out a careful programme with the training officers, taking the apprentices in groups of thirty or forty at a time. We were constantly amazed that we had this tremendous opportunity to be in regular contact with so many who were otherwise completely out of touch with the Church.

With limited time, and given the scale of the rest of the shipyards around us, we began to be concerned that though this work was valuable and important, we were unable to do many other things in the yard that we would have wished. We were delighted, therefore, to find that a local minister, Graham Blount, was able to share with us in this work. Within the Glasgow team we soon recognised there was a distinct sphere of ministry among young people and so we began to explore the possibility of finding the means to appoint a person to do this work as a specialism. We approached Strathclyde Region's Education Department, the Roman Catholic Church in Glasgow, the Congregational, Episcopal, United Free Churches and Iona Community. I managed to get enough money out of these various organisations to fund the appointment of an Industrial Youth Chaplain. The first person appointed was an Episcopal priest, Jim Kay.

When Jim Kay left after three years to take up another appointment, we re-advertised the post. We had always been aware that we had been an entirely male team and so it was very satisfying for us to discover that among the applicants, the best was Alison Bush. She had studied theology at New College but was not ordained. She quickly picked up the work that Jim had been doing, developed a number of new contacts and ways of working with young people, and continued as a very active member of our team until her marriage.

Working Collectively

During 1970, along with a few others committed to industrial mission, I was exploring the need for some more effective ecumenical structure for industrial mission. On 22 June 1970 we formally constituted ourselves the 'Inter-Church Industrial Committee' (ICIC). The members were Ted Lewis of the Church of Scotland, Vincent Cowley of the Roman Catholic Church, David Laing of the Congregational Union, John Banks of the United Free Church, Ted Luscombe of the Scottish Episcopal Church, and Jim Mack of the Methodists, with Miss Anderson of the Church of Scotland's Home Board as treasurer. With some financial assistance from the Glasgow Churches Council, the ICIC became an important ecumenical entity for the ensuing years. Under the auspices of the ICIC we organised industrial mission, ecumenically, in the Glasgow area. The Presbytery of Glasgow's own Church and Industry Committee continued also, but this ecumenical instrument was important to ensure the effectiveness of industrial mission regardless of the different denominations of the Church.

One programme which emerged from the discussions between these two groups and the local chaplains, consisted in a careful consideration of the new Industrial Relations Bill and the Code of Industrial Relations Practice. It was led, each Wednesday, by Jim Kelly, a Church of Scotland elder who lectured on industrial relations at Strathclyde University. Howard Cape led a discussion on the examination of power blocks and Dick Philipps on the question of what is true militancy. An industrial survey was initiated in which we asked kirk sessions in various parts of the city to become involved. The theme, 'A Christian Style of Life in an Industrial City', attracted some 25 people representing a fairly wide range of interests.

I was, however, rather bruised by one event. As full-time industrial chaplains we were very concerned about the effects of industrial change and redundancies. We wondered what ought to be the response of the Church. We felt something should be produced which would help ministers see the pastoral problems associated with redundancy. I wrote a pamphlet called *Redundancy – An Urgent Pastoral Situation,* and I spoke to the Presbytery of Glasgow during the Home Mission report. Out of this two conferences were authorised by the presbytery, one of which was specifically for ministers. Each received the booklet and an invitation to meet the Controller of the Department of Employment and Productivity in Scotland, Mr J S McKenzie. The pastoral situation was to be discussed at a Tuesday morning meeting in Anderston Parish Church. I was astounded and saddened when only the Convener of the Home Mission Committee, Mr McKenzie, Sandy Ryrie, and I, attended. My notes say, 'Needless to say it took me some time today to get over this. The only cure was a spell in a factory and I did good work in MacLaren Controls'. Sandy Ryrie and I then had a long conversation about the advisability of even attempting to work through the Church. We had received many disappointments and there seemed to be a total inability to see faith other than in Church terms.

In the early 70s, the Glasgow Christian Council had become more or less defunct, but under the initiative of the ICIC a series of meetings with them was jointly convened. These were held monthly at the YMCA in Bothwell Street in Glasgow. Some 37 ministers, deaconesses and lay people from a broad spectrum of denominations met, all of whom were actively involved in various aspects of Christian mission in and around the city. We discussed co-ordinating various voluntary and social service activity; and we discussed the Sissons Report – a social study of Church membership in Falkirk. These gatherings developed a strong co-operative spirit of Christian concern to tackle some of the issues of the city in an ecumenical manner.

During that same period, the ICIC and the industrial mission team made a survey of the deployment of industrial mission in Glasgow and some of its obvious gaps. The resources were not great. There was the Church and Industry Committee with 16 members, including trade unionists and officials, managers, presbytery elders and ministers and one full-time chaplain (myself). Jim Mack and David Laing gave a considerable part of their time, as did also John Potter, to part-time chaplaincy. These constituted the core team. In March 1973 John Potter was commissioned as a full-time chaplain in succession to Sandy Ryrie. In addition, twelve part-time chaplains visited Weir Pumps, Gartcosh Steel Works, British Steel, Clyde Port Authority, Glasgow Corporation Transport, Collins, Govan Shipbuilders, MacLaren Controls, Anderson Mavor and British Rail (Queen Street, Central, Larkfield,

General Terminus, Smithylye, Bellahousten, Bridgeton, Buchanan House, and St Rollox), Rank Hovis, Howdens, and Templetons.

By the mid-70s the background structure of industrial mission, both nationally and locally, was fairly well established. The Church and Industry Committee met in Edinburgh five times a year. Because it met in the morning, attendance was largely limited to industrial missioners, some ministers, and a number of retired lay men. Meetings were uninspiring, little more than a reporting back to members on the progress of the work undertaken in the field. Monthly meetings of the full-time team continued to be important, both as a support group for each of us individually, and as a means of clarifying issues and trends within industrial society. The nature of our relationship was always relaxed, informal and personally supportive. George Wilkie was a natural and unobtrusive leader, very thoughtful and reflective, who listened carefully, asked good questions and made helpful contributions. In the broader British context, the Industrial Mission Association (IMA) continued to develop its networks and George Wilkie attended regularly as our representative.

The visit to the Glasgow team of Bill Wright, the team leader of Teeside Industrial Mission, proved to be a significant event. He strongly emphasised the need for a team like ours to clarify its aims. Without acceptance of them there could be difficulties. Team objectives must come out of the aims and should be seen to do so. He strongly recommended the Coverdale method of undertaking the task.

Coverdale training includes techniques of problem-solving and personal interaction. Affecting the structures of industry by making contact and winning the trust of key people in industry, on both sides of the management-trade union line, was the main thrust of the Teeside team. Their approach was highly professional and they had considerable contact with industry.

Bill Wright's emphasis on aim setting encouraged me to enroll for a one-week course in Coverdale Training. It was held at the Chesters School of Management Training, then part of Strathclyde University. I fed back to the team what I had learned and for a number of years thereafter we operated the Coverdale method in our team meetings. This undoubtedly gave us sharpness. It increased our motivation, helped to clarify aims, and gave us a very effective working method. Essentially it recognises that if half a dozen people sit down to discuss, they may often believe they have reached agreement yet end up with half a dozen different aims. The Coverdale method begins with aims being set up on a flip chart, argued over, modified and changed, until everyone finally agrees exactly what the aim is. To fulfil that aim, objectives are set and the question asked: *What has to be done?* This is followed by a time of ingathering of information – data, assistance, already available material, *etc.* The action programme is set out detailing who does what, by what time, and by what measure of success. A review procedure follows. While the complete method is difficult to describe succinctly, it contributed greatly to our team work. Our occasional visitors then often remarked on our professionalism.

One of the most interesting and valuable ingredients of our programme at this period was what we called the 'meal meetings'. Each of us in our various industrial locations knew individuals whose counterparts were in other companies. We decided to bring these together in groupings appropriate to the task they undertook in industry. The problem with Glasgow was its sheer size. People were unwilling to return for an evening meeting in the city after going home at the end of a hard working day. We decided therefore to invite people to meet us immediately after work. We gathered at 5.30 pm until around 6 pm in our office in Elmbank Street; we adjourned to the little restaurant, the 'Rimini' run by Peter Ritcy, below the office, where we had a meal and talk, after which we returned for a very short period to the office. In this way we were able to range over a wide variety of subjects with well informed people. There was always a healthy interaction between ourselves, the team, and the various groups we met. These groups included economists, personnel directors, trade union officials, shop stewards, company medical officers, and others. Another team activity that year was the preparation of the Radio Clyde Service for Mayday in which men and women drawn from our various industrial locations participated. During this year, also, we made a sustained study of Marxism as it affected industrial relations and industrial life in Scotland. In addition I held at our home at Victoria Road a theological evening, with a number of Glasgow theologians and industrial people. We often had visitors to team meetings held in Elmbank Street every second Friday morning. Those invited were asked to arrive at 12.30 and share a working lunch with us. The recently retired president of the AEU, Sir Gavin Laird, was one of them.

In 1974, after a House of Commons report on pay relativities, a careful study of relativities was made by the Church and Industry Committee. The general question of the relative worth of various work activities and their remuneration was studied. Thirteen people formed a core group and we held many discussions with others. In March 1974 we produced a paper based upon the comments of managers, trade unionists and others in Glasgow, entitled *Reflections and Relativities*. Later Stewart Borthwick, the highly popular and effective part-time chaplain at Singers, Clydebank, and myself prepared a report for the National Church and Industry Committee on the role and place of multi-nationals in Scotland.

Another very useful study was that of the work of foremen and supervisors in Scottish industry. We attended courses on supervision organised by the Industrial Society, and prepared questions which we used to elicit answers from a wide variety of people in supervisory jobs. We held a number of meetings with groups of foremen, both in our own office and also in places of work, such as Govan Shipbuilders and British Rail. A useful leaflet, *Foreman: Forgotten Man*, was produced. Hamish Montgomery, who worked as a counsellor at the Tom Allan Centre in Elmbank Street, Glasgow, and who had often designed very effective cartoons for *Worklife,* the newspaper of industrial mission in Scotland, was invited to do a cartoon showing the 'Wee Gaffer', as he was called, under pressure of his many responsibilities. That cartoon is now widely known and still raises a smile (see Appendix on page 141).

Since we were aware of our dependence upon each other, and our dependence on the grace of God in our ministry, we engaged in a prayer discipline which was important to us individually and for our team meetings. On occasion we had what we called a 'team agape meal'. Since our team included Frank Kennedy, a Catholic priest, we did not have Eucharist as such, but we did share bread in prayerful communion.

During 1975 the local Glasgow team worked exceptionally well together and produced two short reports of the work. The team consisted of John Potter, Frank Kennedy, Graham Blount, Harold Clarke and myself, together with the chaplains in engineering, British Steel, British Rail, Glasgow Passenger Transport Executive and Shipbuilding. The first annual report of our activities reported on training courses with young workers and apprentices, the Glasgow Industrial Alcoholism Unit, the Shipbuilding Today survey, the future of work study, the lunch meeting with employees of city firms, round table industrial groups, and conferences and consultations entitled 'Why Industrial Mission is a Must'. The second report, *The Churches' Service to Industry*, was sent to the companies in which we operated, to some twelve trade unions and to all of the participating churches. The report began with some theological background before looking at the aims of industrial mission. It listed our activities in industry as chaplaincy visitation, evening consultations, training department courses, work on unemployment, industrial training, transport policy, contact with chambers of commerce and trades councils, publications, and the Industrial Alcoholism Unit. It also described our work with the churches, including our work with ministers and priests in a series of day consultations, our Four Congregation Project, a slide tape presentation for the churches, student training, radio and TV broadcasts, and Industrial Mission Gatherings. The report also referred to team training and team structure.

In May 1978, the *Evening Times* ran a feature entitled 'Clydeside's Very Special Union'. A half page picture of Frank Kennedy and myself in Scotstoun

Marine was accompanied by the words, 'In a drab little room in Elmbank Street five men cluster round a table munching cheese rolls and sipping tea – a working lunch, but not the prawn cocktail of the slick city executive. This is the Church at work .... They are here,' it continued, 'because they have a vision about Christianity, that it can help people and that it can make use of us in a working environment. They are united in a common cause.' Rosemary Long, the writer, said, 'Any one of them will launch into an enthusiastic analysis on worker management relations, pre-retirement, trends in industry, and industrial alcoholism, at the drop of a hat, because they care about all these things and the men around them. Their vestries are greasy machine rooms and fitting shops. They don't expect a congregation but the message gets across'.

The Glasgow team spent some time considering a number of issues, both topical and important, which required attention from industrial mission. These issues were, of course, already being discussed in many other quarters, but we believed that if industrial mission was to have any bite we must also be discussing them and exposing them to theological clarification. The chaplains' group, the Inter-Church Industrial Committee and the Glasgow presbytery committee, were all involved.

We considered the purpose, aims and goals of industry and our purpose as individuals within industry; power in industry today; the power of the shop floor, the immense power of large corporations, and the emerging power of white collar unionism. We studied the Industrial Relations Bill and thought it would be useful to clarify what the Bill actually said and compare it with the previous Donovan Report on industrial relations. We studied some of the factors affecting women at work, including the problems associated with equal pay. We looked at the question of shop floor militancy and, in a redundancy pamphlet, mentioned the need to question undue militancy. Other issues included industrial democracy, honesty, race relations in industry, the future for apprenticeships, and the effect of shift work for community and social life.

I do not have all of the papers relating to the study of those issues, but one study group on codes of industrial practice had 14 participants. These included Jim Muirhead of the Confederation of British Industry (CBI), Alastair Littlejohn, personnel manager of United Biscuits, Alastair MacFarlane, group manager at William Teacher, Jim Wales of the personnel department of the Scottish Co-operative Wholesale Society (SCWS), Bill Clarke, personnel manager at Sternes, and David Low of personnel training at Sir William Arrols. There were also five trade unionists: Jim Nimmo a full-time official of the Boilermakers Society, Howard Cape, an executive council member of the National Association of Local Government Officials (NALGO), Bill Brodie of ASTMS, Eddie Flannigan of the Amalgamated Engineering Workers Union (AEWU) as it was then, and Harry Davis of ASTMS.

Spreading the Message of Industrial Mission

Cameron Wallace at one stage in the development of the work in the lower
reaches of the Clyde, used to say there were some weeks in which, for three
or four days at a time, the only glimpse he had of the shipyard, where he
was chaplain, was as he passed it on the train on his way to address another
meeting. We all felt it important, not only to be heavily involved in the industry scene, but to try and share some of the sense of mission with the rest of
the Church. All ministers whose ministry has stretched over a few decades,
must look back with amazement at the enormous number of meetings they
have addressed. In industrial mission we were invited to a great variety of
meetings of organisations and, though I cannot recall much of what I said, and
I certainly do not have many notes of those addresses, I do know I must
have been speaking about industrial mission in every corner of Glasgow and
the surrounding area. The transition from school to work, and the role of the
churches, seemed, at first, to be an attractive and important sphere to address.
Experience gained with apprentices illumined my own thinking and I gladly
accepted invitations, such as addressing some three hundred youngsters at
Riverside School. In 1968 I had prepared for the Glasgow Battalion of the
Boys' Brigade a twenty page booklet on the theme of work, although this was,
in my opinion, rather more of an educational task than the core of my job.

From my records there was one period where I visited seven or eight min-
isters' fraternals, including the Church of the Nazarene Ministers' Fraternal.
During the same period I contributed to kirk session conferences with John
Miller of Castlemilk, John Cook at Easterhouse, and with Jim Matheson,
then the Convener of the Church of Scotland's Board of Stewardship. I also
took part in a conference in Ayr, addressed the Glasgow Office Bearers
Society, spoke at a conference at Claremont Church East Kilbride Men's
Association, and at a lunch group at Wellington Church, and many others.

Another cluster included the ministers' fellowship at Perth, the Paisley
Fraternal, apprentices attending the Livingston Motech (an industrial training
centre), the Management Research Group of Strathclyde University, the
Port Glasgow Elders' Conference, the Presbytery of Glasgow, a lecture at
Trinity College (part of the University of Glasgow) and several Men's Groups
and Women's Guilds. I recall being very depressed after a visit to a men's club
at Newarthill where, after two hours of hard-going against some bigotry
about race and little understanding of the role of the Church in society, I
concluded that the Church, for many, was little more than a club.

In the winter of 1976/77, ICIT arranged two or three visits a week to
Church organisations with what was called 'The Church Package'. It was
designed to raise the awareness of members of Church organisations about

the importance of linking faith with the world of work. There was much interest, especially as many knew nothing of industrial mission or industrial chaplains. Our discussions about work and the role of Christians ranged widely, but Church and industry still lived in two separate worlds. We visited a number of congregations, where we preached on the Sunday morning and held conferences in the afternoon. On some occasions, laymen from the Church and Industry Committee participated along with the team of full-time chaplains. During this year the team also continued to organise day consultations with ministers, to encourage them to think into the work-life situations of their members. This we did, for example, during 1976 at Mosspark, Cardonald, Ibrox and Paisley.

The Industrial Mission Trust

Early in the 70s, when it appeared that the Church might well be facing an 'economic blizzard', the then General Secretary of the Home Board of the Church of Scotland, Dr Horace Walker, discussed with George Wilkie, the Secretary of the National Church and Industry Committee and Organiser of Industrial Mission, the question of industry supporting industrial mission. George discussed the matter with leading industrialists and trade unionists who agreed to form an Industrial Mission Trust. The Trust was launched in 1972 and gained charitable status from the Inland Revenue. Annually, thereafter, the Trustees made an appeal to industry. They pointed out that the churches had committed resources of money and staff to serve the needs of people in industry and the Trust was there to allow others in companies and trade unions, who recognised the value and significance of the Church's efforts, to give further financial support.

Though never a major charity, the funding produced by the Industrial Mission Trust has in fact been a significant factor in the life of Industrial Mission. The Church of Scotland's Board of National Mission continued to pay stipends, housing and travel expenses, but this left little for any imaginative development of the work. Although the individual Trustees have changed with the passage of time, industrial mission has always been grateful for the managers, the trade unionists and Church representatives who have continued to encourage industry to donate.

Playing our Part in International Workers' Memorial Day

When major industrial accidents take place there are large headlines in the

Press and widespread media coverage of the causes, the effects and the lessons to be learned. There is sympathy for the large number of people affected. Day in day out, however, industrial accidents take place in ones and twos. These go unnoticed by the Press. There is local trauma and sorrow, local investigation into the cause and a determination to avoid a similar situation. But what is not realised is that the sum and total of these incidents adds up to a significant record of injury and death throughout industry. In addition, industrial processes often cause disease and ill health. Work and the creation of wealth has a cost attached to it. Chaplains are aware of something of the risks and dangers of industry. We have all been involved in the aftermath of industrial accidents, and could record our stories of human suffering and grief, of both workmates and colleagues and their families.

The Workers' Memorial Day began in Canada with the twin purpose of remembering those who had died in the workplace, and reminding people of the need to improve health and safety at work. April 28 was chosen, and on this day events have since been organised in many countries in the world including Britain. In Scotland it was developed by Jim Swan of the Lothian Trade Union and Community Resource Centre. Industrial Mission shared in this and a number of events were organised in different parts of Scotland under the joint auspices of the STUC, Edinburgh District Council, SCIM, the Scottish Hazards Campaign Group, and the Lothian Trade Union and Community Resource Centre.

It is still an uphill struggle to bring to public attention the hazards of industry. In 1992 and 93 I arranged for a commemorative tree-planting and plaque-placing in Princes Street Gardens, Edinburgh. Representative groups of workers came. Some laid wreaths, a piper from the Lothian Police Pipe Band played 'The Flowers of the Forest', and a short service was held, all of which was covered by TV. Similar events have now taken place in Bathgate, Bonnyrigg, Falkirk and Haddington, together with memorial lectures in Edinburgh and Dundee.

One report of the Health and Safety Executive estimated that industrial accidents cost employers between £4bn and £5bn each year. The human cost is the theme of the Memorial Day. Its message is: 'Remember the Dead and Fight for the Living.' In the UK, 450 people are killed in accidents at work each year, but tens of thousands are disabled and many more made unwell by industrial processes. In its report to the General Assembly the Church of Scotland, the Church and Industry Committee has placed these facts before the Church, but action must be taken by all of us.

CHAPTER 7

Contributing to Education

Extra Mural Department Programmes

IT is difficult to recall what triggered the idea of attempting to arrange, through the Extra Mural Department of the University of Glasgow, a number of courses which would support the development of industrial mission. It certainly was a wise decision and instrumental in making quite a number of people aware of the importance of this part of the Church's work. Lecturers included Willie Robertson, the Director of the Scottish Council Development and Industry, who addressed industry's need for purpose and meaning; and Alan Gay, the Director of the Chester's School of Management Training, who lectured on ethics and industrial relations. Professor Alan Galloway spoke about the Christian Doctrine of Work, and the worker priest movement was recalled by Father Nelson of the Roman Catholic Church in Glasgow. A Catholic view of the Church's role in industrial society was given by Father Charles Prigeon SJ, while Sandy Ryrie gave some practical suggestions about the Church's role in industry.

A second course, called 'The Clergy in Industrial Society', was designed for ministers and priests, to make them more aware of the factors affecting men and women at work. Topics included: 'The Shop Floor – Problems and Terminology', 'Organisation and Protection of the Working Man' and 'The Role of Management'. Others were: 'The Criteria of Christian Involvement', 'Social Justice', 'The Industrial Training Act' and 'Directions and Choices for Industrial Society – the Church's Role'.

These two courses were surprisingly well attended. Some 45 ministers and priests came to the clergy course, and thirty people regularly attended on the Wednesday evening. For seven years thereafter I arranged, along with my colleagues, similar courses, and they became an important ingredient of industrial mission in Glasgow. The friendships which developed through these were instrumental in establishing a good base for industrial mission. Frank Kennedy, then a young priest working in Yoker, came to the clergy course. He was immediately interested and was soon persuaded to become involved in industrial mission. He became my closest working colleague in Glasgow and a tremendous asset to the whole of industrial mission until he left for Church work in South America. His book, *God's Working People,* was a valuable contribution to our work. The industrial mission of that era would never have been the same without Frank Kennedy's understanding, wisdom and humour.

For seven years we arranged similar additional courses – on a Monday morning for ministers and priests, and mid-week for lay people. 'The Church and Change in an Urban Industrial Setting', 'The Theological Motivations of an Urban Industrial Ministry', 'Scottish Industry Today', 'Trade Unions Today', 'The Political and Pastoral Problems of Unemployment' and 'Ministry in a Changing Scotland', were some of the subjects covered. The courses for lay people were quite well attended, both at the University and on occasion at Community House, but when we moved them to more peripheral areas, such as Lochend School in Easterhouse, fewer people came. Nevertheless, these Extra Mural Department courses allowed several hundred people to reflect on the issues affecting industrial society and the contribution of the Christian Gospel to them.

Membership of the Glasgow Rotary

Shortly after my appointment as industrial chaplain in Glasgow, Duncan Campbell, well-known as the churchman of the *Evening Citizen*, took me as a guest to the Glasgow Rotary. It met on a Tuesday at the Grosvenor Hotel opposite the Central Station. The membership consisted of some three hundred men representing a most diverse cross-section of Glasgow life. Rotary believed the club should consist of at least one person from each industry, sector of commerce, profession and occupation. Service to the community, to wider society, and to international affairs, were its aims. It also encouraged good standards of professional and business life. I accepted the invitation to join and for seven years participated in its activities.

As chairman of the Vocational Service Committee, I and others strove to ensure that this committee would be the motivating committee of the Glasgow Rotary. Rotarians were reminded of the need to serve others. We focused on the Rotarian and his Customer, the Rotarian and his Competitor, the Rotarian and his Seller, and the Rotarian and his Employee. Membership of the Rotary was helpful in a number of ways, not least for the weekly interaction, frequently of a friendly argumentative nature, with men in senior positions in different organisations. After spending a morning on the shop floor of McLaren Controls, for example, on occasion countering the mis-conception of some of the workers on the role of management, I would lunch with Rotarian managers, countering their mis-conceptions of the shop floor. The same Glasgow accent expressed totally different views of the industrial world which someone in the privileged position of an industrial chaplain could see from a different angle.

Sunday Evening Study Groups

Sunday evening study groups in my house were an important support to me, and an opportunity of reflecting on the work of industrial mission. A group of ten managers and trade unionists, helped by a theologian, John Cumpsty, met fortnightly in my home for two years. John had worked in a similar way with industrial mission in the north east of England. We discussed situations arising from the experience of group members, including ethical and moral questions. For example, Tom Evans, managing director of a large engineer-ing company, spoke of the dilemmas facing someone in his position. On another occasion we discussed the response of drawing office trade union corresponding members to a colleague who refused to join the union. At other times, we looked at more fundamental themes – such as dehumanisation in industry. The meaning of Christian witness in the workplace was never far from our thoughts. Afterwards I typed a summary which was sent out to the participants. At the following meeting we began with a theological reflection by John Cumpsty on what had been said at the previous meeting. Altogether it was a most educative experience.

Work with City Centre Groups

At Renfield: St Stephen's church, in the city centre of Glasgow, Angus Turner, the Associate Minister, led groups which tried to look at the city from a Christian perspective. These, however, largely comprised elderly members of the congregation. I joined him and we invited Hamish Montgomery, the leader of the nearby Tom Allan Centre for social work, to participate. We invited a diverse group of people from different levels of responsibility with-in city offices, four from three separate companies, to a meeting over a buffet lunch each Wednesday. We intended consulting them about their experience of the practical and emotional problems of city life. We hoped to shape the programmes of the city centre churches to match the needs of the office population. So we contacted the Housing Co-operative, the Scottish Brick

Company, the Glasgow Libraries, the Inland Revenue, C F Lillies, the Royal Bank, the Social Security Office, Trerons, National Provincial, the Dental Hospital, Phillips Petroleum, Clyde Port Authority, and others. These were more successful than the previous meetings.

In addition we ran two series of eight Wednesday lunchtime discussions. On each occasion the chaplains were joined by twelve people from three different companies. Questions were raised, such as: *What is it like for you to work in the city? What is one positive feature for you about living and working in the city of Glasgow?* and *What is one negative feature about living and working in the city of Glasgow?* We also asked them to give us an idea of how they expected the churches to respond to the needs of city people and city life. We would ask them to write down one word which expressed their feelings about the city. We gave a brief description of the churches' current work in the city.

From the beginning, replies were charted so that everyone saw their own contribution. The 'one word' question got replies such as: 'Rush ... people being glum ... ritual ... lost in crowd ... routine ... lack of communication ... stress ... strain ... agreeable ... inward looking ... enjoyable ... stimulating ... anonymous ... frustrating ... demanding ... dynamic ... pressurised.' On another occasion we noted on the chart: 'the need to overcome isolation ... not knowing where meeting can take place in the city centre ... the provision of music in the city centre ... the arrangement of competitions or activities between city centre companies ... the holding of seminars on ideas of common interest.'

This process I found stimulating. Although it was time-consuming to arrange the meetings, I felt they had the potential to become a very useful tool for bringing people into contact with each other. We found that people, even in a large city, lived isolated lives. Many travelled by train, bus or car, in isolation, arrived at their work, and met surprisingly few people. We took satisfaction from the knowledge that at each gathering 15 or so people shook hands as strangers, sat down to lunch, had worthwhile conversation, and left knowing much more about each other's views, attitudes and hopes.

Following this experience the City Centre Christian Group decided to offer its services to Strathclyde Region. A number of senior directors of several of the departments of the Region met the city centre Church people over lunch, with a view to sharing insights and looking at how friendliness and human growth could be maintained at the heart of the city. We explained that the city churches had their normal parish tasks to perform, but they were aware of not being sufficiently prepared to serve the thousands who worked in the city centre. We said there was no dividing wall between the domestic and working lives of people. They retain human needs in spite of the sometimes dehumanising effect of city life and large organisations.

We also provided a brochure for the personnel managers of many city centre businesses. In it we listed a number of Church resources to which they could turn. These included the chaplaincy service of industrial mission, the Tom Allan Centre, the local churches, the Employee Counselling Service (the new name for the Industrial Alcoholism Unit), and a number of other organisations in the city centre which would be of value to companies.

Work and Marriage

I prepared material for congregational discussion groups on the subject of work and marriage. We encouraged ministers to invite four or five people to meet around three points of common interest, their membership of a congregation, their Christian belief, and their job. We produced background material with the quotation:

> *Armed with their certificate of respectability, blessed by their minister and protected by their mortgages, the married couple slowly eat each other alive, use friends, lovers and casual visitors only as weapons in their total warfare, finally sinking exhausted together because the contest has made each so unattractive that no one else will put up with them.*

We asked if this was what marriage was *really* like. We talked about work and home, mid-life crisis, money, the sandwich years, and house husbands.

The Industrial Alcoholism Unit

Mis-use of alcohol was one of the biggest problems for industry in the West of Scotland. Companies of all sizes suffered from the consequences of alcohol abuse. People were ruining their own lives and those of their families. The Monday syndrome of early pass-outs and early afternoon departures, were all too familiar. Trade unionists and managers were often in constant frustrated inter-action over one case after another. There were frequent industrial disputes over the problem. The financial cost to companies was incalculable and no one seemed to have an answer. Chaplains tried their best to help individuals. I remember one good friendly man at Davy United who was obviously killing himself with drink. He had lost contact with his family and lived in one of the model lodging houses at Glasgow Cross. I took him to Alcoholics Anonymous (AA) and, although he had a couple of regressions, he eventually remained sober. Two years later in Glasgow's George Square, he shouted to draw my attention. He was in a business suit, looking healthy and fit, working as a messenger with one of the city stores.

In the canteen in Govan Shipbuilders one day, big Stevie approached me. This broad-shouldered, muscular man had just been suspended from work again. I took him home to his house in Govan Road, but went back for him in the evening only to discover him in a terrible condition. I got hold of Archie of Alcoholics Anonymous. Three hours later we managed to get him admitted to the Southern General Hospital. The fact that this one individual case took that amount of time, and there were thousands more in a similar situation, indicated that something really had to be established to deal with this problem. I raised the matter with a number of managers and trade union officials. I also discussed it with the personnel director of British Rail and with drivers and guards. We all felt the need of a new way of dealing with this old problem.

Somewhat tentatively, I convened three conferences in 1975 on alcohol mis-use at work. The first was held in the Renfield Centre to which twelve industrial relations directors and managers, together with their conveners of shop stewards, were invited. Along with Archie G of AA and a friend, Dr Munro, we explored the need for a better system than that currently in use. There was a greater interest than I had expected. We followed this with a second meeting, held in the Glasgow City Chambers. Representatives of Rolls Royce management and shop stewards attended with considerable enthusiasm. Finally, we convened, at Chester School of Management Training in Bearsden, a larger conference of 150 people from a similar group of personnel and trade union representatives. It was held jointly in the names of Industrial Mission and the Glasgow Council of Alcoholism. There was no intention on the part of industrial mission to establish a separate organisation and so we were delighted when the Glasgow Council on Alcoholism expressed willingness to appoint an Industrial Director to whom referrals could be made. Unfortunately, within three months of the beginning of the scheme, the Glasgow Council of Alcoholism closed it because of a lack of money. We then went ahead and set up the Industrial Alcoholism Unit.

The development of the Unit, later to be called the Employee Counselling Service, arose directly from our work with industry.

Companies all over the West of Scotland soon knew of its existence and forty people a month were being referred to it. The Committee of Management's task is to raise funds to make sure the full-time staff are adequately remunerated. Committee members represent the Scottish Trade Union Congress (STUC), the CBI, the Institute of Personnel Development, the

Greater Glasgow Health Board, the Council Social Work Department, and others. Industrial Mission continues to play a leading role and, of the full-time chaplains, John Potter, Angus Turner and I have all represented industrial mission. Professional evaluation of the results indicates a high level of success. Quite recently the organisation was the first of its kind in the West of Scotland to receive the coveted Investors in People award. Since its inception, thousands of people have had the opportunity of a new beginning with an escape from illness, and perhaps loss of job.

The Employee Counselling Service

I would have been amazed back in 1976, having initiated the Industrial Alcoholism Unit, that twenty years later not only would it still exist, but that it would still be developing. Both managers and trade unionists appreciate the promptness with which troubled employees are helped and the professional manner in which reports are made to them. Clients appreciate the essential confidentiality of the counselling. Inevitably the Management Committee and the staff have changed with the passage of time. Thanks are due to past managers of the Unit – Archie Graham, Andy Cameron, and Angus Mac-Farlane; and now to Pauline Bryan and the many who have given of their time freely in acting as members of the Committee of Management. Though dealing with employees with drink-related problems has always been a main activity, personnel managers are increasingly referring people with other problems related to drugs, bereavement and post-traumatic stress, amongst others.

In 1990 the name was changed from the Industrial Alcoholism Unit to the Employee Counselling Service (ECS) to indicate the wider range of service provided. Staff training and professionalism was emphasised and more training seminars provided at the request of companies. Publicity leaflets were produced both for individuals and companies. At an international conference on alcohol, a presentation was made by the ECS. In response to an invitation from Poland, Strathclyde Regional Council invited the ECS to assist and the Service Manager went to Poland for that purpose. After many visits to the offices of the Employee Counselling Service, a similar organisation based on our methods was set up in London.

CHAPTER 8

Involved
with the Unemployed

WHILE industrial mission focuses on people in employment, it cannot ignore the constant threat of redundancy and unemployment. How much time should be given to this and should the focus of industrial mission change? How much should be left to other agencies of the Church, the parish ministry, congregations, presbyteries, boards of social responsibility, and the General Assembly of the Church of Scotland?

In response, the Glasgow team gathered groups of unemployed people from labour exchanges. We stood at the door of a labour exchange and spoke to people as they went in and out. We gave them verbal and printed invitations to meetings about unemployment. These were held in Woodside Hall, Maryhill Trades Club, St Francis-in-the-East Church Hall in Bridgeton, and elsewhere. They were addressed by well-known people in industry and the unions and from newspapers and television. The TV journalist, Jimmy Gordon, later to become Chief Executive of Radio Clyde, came; as did Hugh Morran, the Director of Scotland West Industrial Promotion Group, John Reidford, the Secretary of the Glasgow's Trade Council, Father Gerry Fitzpatrick from Bridgeton, John Lang, a minister in Bridgeton, officials from the Department of Unemployment, and many others.

In Maryhill, where sixty attended the original meeting, a small group continued to meet together in the Maryhill Methodist Church Hall. This was probably the earliest job club in the city. The *London Times* wrote an article on our work under the title 'The Holy Alliance With The Unemployed'.

In the early '70s, the Glasgow Church and Industry Committee published a number of leaflets on unemployment. The sharp style of *Redundancy in the West of Scotland* produced a response from management and unions. It argued for the removal of stigma from the person made redundant and that older people be given employment chances. It asked companies to be honest in their statements of intent, that public enquiry into large closures be mandatory, automatic militancy be questioned, that trade unionists condemn selfishness, and that the Government, *any* government, must accept greater responsibility for regional employment.

It sounds old fashioned now, but at the time we believed we were making an appropriate Christian response. It was read because we were known to be working outside the churches in the world of business and industry. We produced the leaflets in large numbers and gave them out at many different meetings. We also urged local authorities, central Government and others, to take a number of practical steps to help the unemployed.

We ourselves encouraged ministers in small teams, to give part of a morning each week, from spring to autumn, to meet with people at labour exchanges. Thereby we investigated an appropriate ministry to the unemployed, drew up a list of their experiences, and considered an appropriate response from the Church.

After notifying the ministers of the Presbytery of Glasgow, four teams were set up. Ian Goring led one at Easterhouse – a large housing estate on the edge of Glasgow – along with John Cook, Alister Moodie, Russell Barr and Robin Watt. One at Anniesland included Bob Duncan, Stuart Lang, Bill Christman and Graham Blount. Colin Caskie and others formed another at Govan and Hillington. At Parkhead and Bridgeton, Erik Cramb and Robin McHavey, Gavin Elliot, Ian Lang and others, took part. These ministers were already sensitive and were attempting, in various ways, to relate to unemployed people and the issues. Those most in need of being reminded of this aspect of ministry failed to respond to the invitation and lost an opportunity of direct contact with unemployed people.

Later, with a group of ministers from urban priority parishes, we explored initiatives they might take in relation to unemployed people.

We were all impressed with Russell Barr's account of how he sat for three weeks, at times he had announced in advance, waiting for unemployed people to come to the church hall – without anyone coming. His persistence was rewarded. Eventually one or two, then others, came to him. Finally a group was established on terms which the people themselves, mainly young people, wanted. He wanted to support them while they took the decisions.

Youth Opportunity Programmes

A number of Government programmes, administered by the Manpower Services Commission (MSC), were developed in the '70s. They were designed to deal with the increasing problem of unemployment, both among young people and adults. In 1976, for instance, there was a conference convened by the Scottish Community Education Centre and the MSC, in the Grosvenor Hotel, Glasgow, on the Youth Opportunities Programme (YOP) and the Special Temporary Employment Programme. These had emerged from the main proposals of the Holland Working Party Report, *Young People and Work.* YOPs were to be introduced in early 1977. The conference examined the proposed YOP in detail, considered possible developments and methods of operation, and identified a potential role for the voluntary sector in implementing the community service component.

For a number of years thereafter Industrial Mission tried to stimulate within the churches, and elsewhere, appropriate involvement with the MSC. After the end of the MSC, I wrote a chapter of a book on the MSC in Scotland, entitled 'The MSC and the Churches', which recorded the Church's involvement with the MSC over a 15 year period.

I was a member of the Glasgow South District Manpower Committee of the Employment Service Agency, chaired for a while by Alec Ferrie until his promotion to a post in London. At these meetings, employers, trade unionists, and others from the wider community, were brought together. They considered the implementation of Government policy in employment training, industrial training boards, the development of work experience and job creation. Officials regularly reported on employment and labour deployment in the district.

The Church and Industry Committee of the Presbytery of Glasgow reminded the presbytery of the opportunities arising both for the church and for the young through Community Industry, another aspect of the work of the MSC. Community Industry was to 'care for the sparrows, but not the eagles': that is, those suffering from disadvantage as a result of neglect and indifference in their former years. Work could be done for congregations under the supervision of responsible craftsmen, simultaneously providing work for youngsters. Many congregations benefited from Community Industry.

Redundancy and the Redundancy improvement Scheme (RISK)

Towards the end of the 1970s it was clear that people about to be made redundant needed help. Thousands were being made redundant. Companies, large and small, were laying people off, some after blazing publicity, others silently and overnight. For some the experience was appalling. Often very little was being done to assist people through this traumatic process. When people normally retire they are, in a number of ways, prepared for this major change in their lives. They have plans for their retirement and their use of time. They have thought about the financial implications. Retirement is talked about openly and hopefully and, in some cases, there are courses which people could find useful. But what happens to the person who loses his or her job before normal retirement? There is often no preparation, only rejection, loss of dignity and identity, sometimes with inadequate financial provision.

In 1980 we asked representatives of the CBI, the STUC, Strathclyde Regional Council's Education Department, the Glasgow University Extra Mural and Psychology Departments, the Engineering Industry Training Board and others, to meet with industrial chaplains. This group agreed that a process be set up which would make it possible, even normative, for people to be given appropriate help in the event of being made redundant.

With the co-operation of Strathclyde's Education Department, a new organisation was formed to help people in employment about to be made redundant. A course dealing with six important areas of life after redundancy was prepared for use, in company time, *before* people were made redundant. The first course manager called the project Redundancy Improvement Scheme (RISK). In 1984, of the ten thousand people made redundant in Strathclyde, nearly four thousand benefited from courses run by RISK.

Many people – bank managers, building society managers, housing specialists, for example – freely gave their time to the courses. Questioning of participants indicated that they were deeply appreciated and regular assessment of course content allowed their continuous improvement. RISK ran for about seven years and although Strathclyde Region, with a short delay, initiated a project along similar lines, it was always a matter of regret to me that the Redundancy Improvement Scheme was not taken up elsewhere.

The MSC and the Church

Many job-related Government schemes were introduced in the 1980s: Job Creation, the Special Temporary Employment Programme, the Youth Opportunity Programme, and so on. Late in the decade, in their Education and Society series, Edinburgh University published, *The Manpower Services Commission in Scotland*. The picture of a crossword on the cover aptly caught the spirit of how people came to regard the variety of special programmes.

The book traced the history of the MSC in Scotland from the perspective of the many organisations closely involved with it. Chapters were written by those who had worked with schemes in education, industry, local authorities, and the STUC. As already mentioned, I wrote the chapter on the 'MSC and the Church'. With the permission of Edinburgh University Press and the editors, I include here that chapter to illustrate the interaction between industrial mission, the churches in Scotland, and the MSC, during those years.

* * *

THE churches in Scotland have been involved with the MSC almost from its very beginning. The story has been patchy, however, with, in some places, a whole community transformed by the close co-operation of the Church and the MSC, and, in others, very small projects of a simple pastoral and supportive nature.

The schemes that the Church became involved with were largely those which would be categorised under the heading of anti-unemployment initiatives. They were motivated by the need to do something to alleviate the worst effects of unemployment and to provide useful activity. There were reservations about specific programmes, but in general, as one churchman said, 'We have developed a pragmatic attitude to the question of the value of the programmes, recognising that you can always find fault with them, but in the end, for the vast majority of the unemployed these were the only opportunities on offer'.

There were those in the Church who distanced themselves from the programmes, not out of apathy or lethargy, but on principle, believing that they were Government measures which did not go to the heart of the economic and employment realities. This was not, however, a widely-held view. In addition to those in the Church who became actively involved in the initiation and sponsoring and running of schemes, there were many more who gave careful and serious consideration to the possibilities and spent many hours discussing appropriate steps, and yet who were unable to bring into fruition a suitable project. The reasons for this varied: from problems of accommodation, supervision, identification of a project suitable to the area, to the amount of time and effort essential for success.

If there had been no such thing as the MSC, it is hoped that the Church would somehow or other have measured up to the needs of the day and the changing economic realities, but certainly the role and the influence of the MSC upon the Church has been considerable.

All of the main churches in Scotland participated in the various programmes, and were encouraged so to do by their assemblies and hierarchies. In the Roman Catholic Church, however, there was, according to Father William Slaven, 'no policy response through Bishops' Synod and little local involvement'.

One of the problems in making some kind of assessment of the role and influence of the MSC in relation to the work of the Church, is the sheer difficulty of adequate records and statistics. There was no mechanism for ensuring that schemes operated in presbyteries and parishes throughout the country, were recorded centrally by any church. Attempts were made on a number of occasions, but at no point was it ever possible to say that a complete list of all projects had been compiled.

It would be useful if we could measure the role and influence of the MSC against a number of key factors, the time consumption by ministers and office bearers of the churches, the numbers of people employed within projects over the years, the number and type of project undertaken, the amount of MSC funds applied, the benefits experienced by the community which each church sought to serve, the impact upon congregational life and activity; or perhaps, most importantly, the effect on the lives of the people employed within the various projects. Sad to say, there is no effective measure of most of those. It could rightly be said that the people involved from the churches and the MSC were so busy getting on with the job, along with their multifarious other activities of Church and community, that they had no time or inclination to maintain an adequate historical record and analysis.

In 1976, Roger Clarke in Dundee, along with others, initiated the Dundee Council of Churches Training Workshop. This was not the first training workshop in Scotland, but it was the first developed in partnership with the MSC, and this initial project of the churches was highly commended by officials of the MSC. It was regarded as a model because not only did it provide jobs, it pointed to socially useful work which would be needed in the community, and which could supply young people and others with skills for wider application in later life. A very rough measure of the growth of Church involvement with the MSC is provided by occasional listings of Church projects.

In November 1983, for example, following a 'market place', mentioned earlier in this book, and during which Church-related projects were demonstrated, some fifty seven Church-based projects were briefly described. These were both Youth Training Schemes (YTS) and Community Programme (CP) Schemes. There were YTS placements in church eventide homes, at St Ninian's Youth Training Centre and in staffing of play groups, toy libraries, community care and information sharing. Through the CP there was the provision of advice and counselling, alternative employment initiatives, age care, disabled care, community odd jobs, furniture removal, afternoon centres for the unemployed and a resource centre.

In 1986, the General Assembly of the Church of Scotland received an updated list and called for the Church to increase its involvement. Many of these schemes were small in size but dealt with pockets of local need and provided services which otherwise would have been absent from the local scene.

Two projects, which for different reasons are not characteristic, deserve and have had elsewhere a fuller analysis. They are the projects at Buckhaven in Fife and in Gilmerton in Edinburgh. Donald Skinner, the Parish Minister at Gilmerton, first used church resources and buildings, later with MSC funds, to develop the potential of disadvantaged youngsters. Existing before MSC, this project had an important and sometimes profound influence on the six hundred young people trained during the years of the MSC. Donald Skinner used his own engineering background to create a unique training workshop, and under the guidance of highly motivated supervisors, the youngsters developed skills and qualifications in wood-work, metalwork knitwear, art, design, pottery and ceramics. Many became equipped to find work based on those skills.

It is impossible in the space of a few lines to summarise in any adequate way the interaction of the MSC and the community of Buckhaven in Fife. The whole town of Buckhaven and its surrounding communities have been physically and spiritually transformed by the vision of the Revd Dane Sherrard and his kirk session and parish church by co-operation with the MSC.

In all, an astonishing total of 1745 men, women and youngsters had their working lives changed for good, through this project. Whereas local employers had not been attracted by YTS, the local minister and his kirk session were invited by the MSC to consider the Community Programme.

Beginning with the renovation of a church as a Craft and Youth Centre, a team began which was to surprise everyone in the community and indeed in the MSC. Youngsters became hopeful, marriages were stabilised, morale improved, nine hundred people found permanent employment, there was a transfusion of funds to the community from a £40,000 per week pay roll, and, finally, the successful inauguration of an enterprise company marketing tapestry, furniture, and goods produced from silk screen printing, leather tooling, bookbinding and other products. The Economist's report on job creation said 'Buckhaven is held up as a model of how to apply the Community Programme and the Youth Training Scheme to best effect. There are many such schemes, but few where the impact upon the com-munity has been so marked'.

The MSC and the Churches Objectives

Did working with the MSC help the Church meet Church objectives? Many accept that the prime objective of the Church is the proclamation of the gospel for the salvation of individual souls. But the Gospel also involves commitment to the Kingdom of Christ, which includes working for peace and justice in society. Measures which alleviate distress, serve the community, make constructive use of skills, and encourage individuals to develop their own abilities, are undoubtedly objectives worth pursuing. They also reflect the core of the Christian gospel. In this sense, working with the MSC did help the Church meet its own objectives.

Throughout the Church there was a genuine appreciation both of the MSC, as an organisation, and of its area managers and officers. Contact, dialogue and discussion with them, often clarified the appropriate path of action for the churches.

Many congregations did 'go it alone', and quite successfully in certain cases. Others found that the community was more effectively served by working with the MSC. This often involved working with other churches and community groups. These alliances were beneficial and often bore fruit for the Church's task in other areas of life. Where local congregations had been immersed almost entirely in congregational activity, working with MSC programmes brought them a wider grasp of community issues and increased their understanding of social conditions in the parish. This affected the worship and prayers of the Church.

The Church has traditionally cared for the distressed, the elderly and the disadvantaged. Over the years of the MSC the churches shared in many excellent projects serving people within those categories. Without funding from the MSC they would never have got going.

Some Associated Difficulties

The Revd Dane Sherrard who led the large MSC funded project in Buckhaven, said, 'Our relationship with the MSC was not one in which 'problem' was an appropriate word. We both thought of each other as partners'. Others did find difficulties because the aims and objectives of the Church and the MSC were never identical. The MSC frequently made effective use of the concept of partnership, as with the churches and voluntary organisations, but there were obvious differences between the objectives of the MSC and the objectives of the churches. The latter often focused on job creation.

The distinctive aims of churches and the voluntary sector were inadequately understood by many MSC staff. The mechanisms for representation on issues of concern rarely worked to the satisfaction of the Commission's partners. In the early days of the churches' involvement, MSC officers willingly listened to the concerns of the churches and other operating partners. This was very much the philosophy of MSC chairman, Sir Richard O'Brien, who wanted to achieve consensus. As time went on, however, the operating partners were excluded from matters of policy. Decisions and changes to programmes were made with little consultation. There was no attempt to check out in advance the effects of policy shifts, and the operating partners were often brought in after the event.

Local Advisory Boards and Area Manpower Boards occasionally included representatives of the churches and voluntary organisations. The representation was inadequate – especially as they were providing about a third of the community placements. No voice from the voluntary sector systematically percolated through to the Commission. In Scotland there was no Church representative on any national advisory body, and increasingly, the operating partners' concerns were apparently unheeded. Government could change policy, and the MSC issue new guidelines which departmental civil servants had to implement. People involved with churches and voluntary organisations found it difficult to understand the suddenness with which change was made, and even if they had understood, found it difficult to get their less enthusiastic colleagues to accept them.

In the west of Scotland, a frequent complaint was the rapidity of the shifting MSC goal posts. In the east, the complaint differed only in that they became rugby posts!

Inevitably, MSC staff at local level changed over time, but this often had an adverse effect on local partners. The discontinuities caused by staff turn-over, the difficulty of gaining confidence, the newly arrived officer's lack of knowledge of local conditions, all caused difficulties. Church partners frequently felt the MSC to be inflexible. In some areas, where there was a particularly good relationship with an MSC official, this inflexibility could be overcome. Some local officials were most co-operative in not only inter-preting, but perhaps bending the rules, to make it possible for schemes to develop. These mature servants of the Commission were much respected, and the aims of the Commission were as fully implemented under their guid-ance as under the guidance of their less flexible colleagues.

The 'fifty two week rule', after which trainees must leave the programme, was a constant source of complaint. While it was well understood at policy level, at local level it caused unending difficulties for projects. As the Revd Hugh Wylie, of Hamilton Old Church said of Community Programme (CP) staff: 'They were unsure of themselves for a month or two, then they were fine. When they realised the end was in sight, they slumped in efficiency and their time-keeping and enthusiasm dropped away.'

There was an inevitable tension between the aims of local projects, which had been approved by the MSC, and the purposes of the MSC in ensuring a throughput of individuals.

When project organisers had to lay off trainees who, after a year, had gained experience, there was regret, recrimination and complaint, but the rules required these individuals be sacked. Project organisers blamed the fifty two week rule for the mis-use of sickness leave, and for poor perfor-mance. Projects also suffered when the number of people allocated to them suddenly altered. A sudden increase raised problems of expansion; a sudden reduction often required the complete reorganisation of the programme. Church-based project leaders were often irritated by the monitoring process.

In one west coast presbytery, the church elder, a professional engineer, appointed to the MSC scheme on behalf of his church, said, 'MSC officials were very helpful at the beginning of a scheme, but the monitoring process drove you skatty.' The Revd Donald Skinner, whose congregation was heavily involved with MSC projects, has much to say on this subject: 'In the early days the MSC training officers were all tradesmen. I respected them. But what credentials do some of those pen pushers have, on our ability to deliver?' he once complained. Moreover, the MSC identified agencies under whose umbrella many smaller schemes were co-ordinated. These were a mixed blessing. The Revd Iain Matheson said, 'It was the MSC who suggested that we come under an agency two years ago. It freed us certainly from administrative burdens, but produced a superfluity of bosses and resulting confusion for staff and supervisors.'

Some Church groups experienced long periods of uncertainty during the development stage of programmes.

Arranging premises and local funding had to proceed while there was no guarantee of the project being approved. It could take a long time to get projects up and running. Hard pressed parish ministers, elders and Church office bearers, most of whom had full-time occupations, found form-filling and monitoring a frustrating impediment. One presbytery committee proposed a glossary of what they called, 'those damned initials'. In spite of the difficulties Church people were generally satisfied with their relationship with the MSC. They regarded the problems as part of the process of a changing society, and attempts by Government to cope with a difficult economic situation. A number of schemes found it difficult to gain trade union approval.

Understandably trade unions wanted to avoid job substitution. For instance, one Church project which ran for a number of years in local authority premises, was vetted by the National Association of Local Government Officers (NALGO). Reluctantly, they allowed it to proceed. It ended when NALGO pressed for the project and its staff to be taken into the mainline funding of the authority. In some cases there was a lack of understanding on the part of Church people about the role and function of trade unions. Impatience developed over what they saw as unnecessary delay in the granting of permission for obviously valuable projects. A number of projects were delayed for up to a year waiting for trade union approval. Nevertheless, the relationship between churches and trade unions in Scotland was generally good.

What did the Church Learn?

As might be expected, lengthy interaction between the MSC and the churches affected the churches themselves. When the Revd Keith Campbell's congregation in Broughty Ferry, decided to provide day centre care for disabled teenagers in their church halls, they embarked on a lengthy learning experience. Monthly reports of its problems and progress also recorded their growing sensitivity to areas of life of which they might otherwise have been ignorant. People who struggled through the laborious process of discussion, form filling, experimentation, sponsorship and supervision to create viable and useful projects could take pride in contributing to something in which their church might not otherwise have been involved.

Many Church people have some understanding of the spiritual aspect of the Gospel. They can agree that its message must be applied in the world. They applaud the overseas missionary work of the Church and work amongst disadvantaged groups in society. The prospect of placing their own resources of time, effort and properly at the service of the community about them, was an eye-opener for many. They discovered something of the difficulties of community-based Christian action.

There were some outstanding examples of the use of Church premises for MSC schemes, in Anderston Glasgow, St Aidan's Dundee, Hamilton Old, Provanmill, Paisley St Ninian's, Buckhaven and Gilmerton Edinburgh. Congregations and parishes became aware of the impact of the programmes, and with various levels of enthusiasm were willing to accept the inconvenience of the new use of their premises.

The 1986 Church and Nation Report to the General Assembly of the Church of Scotland contained two and a half pages on the Youth Training Scheme (YTS) and the new proposal for a two-year training scheme. It recognised the deficiencies experienced by some young people in the YTS, and welcomed the introduction of the new two year scheme. It urged the Government to improve the quality of the training offered, to consider a substantial improvement in the level of payment, and to encourage employers, to appoint trainees to permanent positions at the end of their training period.

That year the Assembly instructed all presbyteries and congregations to consider actively undertaking projects to create new employment and drew attention to the possibility of MSC funding. Every congregation in the Church of Scotland received a leaflet, The Unemployed – Is there Something We can do?, designed to encourage them to become involved in MSC projects. Many projects already undertaken by congregations were listed together with an estimate of the hundreds of jobs created. It gave a step-by-step guide for congregations that wanted to work with the MSC.

All too few congregations stirred themselves into any adequate activity. Those who had gained experience of establishing projects were frequently asked for guidance and a lot of time was spent on this. Often, however, ideas never resulted in action.

Some congregations even declared their unwillingness to put their resources at the disposal of the community. Some of these had attractive leisure and sports facilities for members of the congregation to use in the evenings or at the weekend. They would have been ideal for unemployed young people, as an adjunct to other MSC activities, but were made unavailable through fear of damage or overuse.

On the other hand, many individuals and groups within the churches experienced a new way of working within their community. Skills available within the congregation were placed at the disposal of others and new skills were developed. Levels of pastoral care were discovered which would not have developed apart from MSC schemes.

The staff of Industrial Mission, through which the churches try to influence worklife, has many contacts with people in industry. Their knowledge and the strength of those contacts enabled them quickly to grasp the best features of the MSC programmes, to understand their importance and to encourage the churches to play an effective part in them. At the same time this did not inhibit critical comment to Government and the MSC from Industrial Mission.

Church representatives served on Area Manpower Boards (AMB). John Potter, the full-time chaplain in Lanarkshire, was an AMB chairman. Alister Goss, another full-time chaplain wrote to me to say, 'Membership of the Board was useful. It enabled us to keep abreast of the debate about changes in the programmes, as well as sharing in the monitoring of work at local level. It would be easy to exaggerate the influence we may have had over the work of the MSC, but I am sure that in a number of instances it was possible to share the delivery of programmes at local level as well as making a contribution to the debate about new programmes.' He was also a member of a nation-wide voluntary organisation which, he said, was able to make recommendations to the MSC which influenced some of its proposals.

Sadly, I have to conclude that the churches were largely unable to influence the MSC. They often found it inflexible. This impression of the MSC's rigidity and apparent unwillingness to be influenced, may not be totally justified. In larger schemes there had to be some give and take, to tailor resources to needs. In Buckhaven, Dane Sherrard and the MSC were able to adapt and be flexible with each other, but others, with considerable experience of operating schemes, found it difficult to get senior MSC officials to meet them for discussion.

The Charities Initiative

In London in the summer of 1985 the Scottish churches were represented at a meeting convened by the Department of Employment. They wanted the churches to share in the new 'charities' initiative'. In addition to the Community Programme, voluntary organisations, including churches, would be given the chance to set up separate projects. There would be a weekly grant for every person employed, from which national insurance contributions would be deducted. Scottish Church representatives involved with MSC programmes rejected the proposal. They felt it was not as good as the existing CP, although Baptist and Methodist churches in Scotland, did make some use of it. It enabled churches to employ individuals outwith involvement in the CP.

The spirit of this story of some 15 years might best be summarised in the words of the Revd Hugh Wylie of Hamilton Old Parish Church, 'Had I known the time it would have taken and the amount of supervision it required of me, I might not have started the projects. But again, I would have done so. It is, in perspective, a small price to pay to be able to give people a start again. That is what matters'.

CHAPTER 9

More
Missioners

On becoming National Organiser

IT was the custom for chaplains annually to review their personal goals and for the team to review its tasks and aims. We reduced this to one A4 page and at the top of mine I always stated my prime aim was to maintain a worthy industrial mission presence in Glasgow. Now in 1980, as National Organiser, I saw that my aim must be to sustain an effective industrial mission in Scotland. This aim could only be fulfilled through the best use of the combined resources of the full-time team, the national and local Church and Industry committees, the local chaplains, and committed lay men and women. I recognised that the work divided into a number of different categories.

The basic task was to service industrial mission. This meant preparing for and carrying out the instructions of the Church and Industry Committee, supporting local industrial chaplains, ensuring continuity when chaplains moved, recruiting new chaplains, and maintaining relationships with Church of Scotland presbyteries and other churches throughout the United Kingdom. It also involved work for other committees of the Church of Scotland – such as the Church and Nation Committee – as well as for the Home Board, preparing for the monthly meetings of the full-time chaplains and processing the decisions made. In fact, the task was largely servicing, processing and initiating.

In Glasgow, since one of my chaplaincies was with British Rail, my colleagues used to describe me occasionally in railway grade terms as 'a running foreman'. The task of that man was to ensure the efficient running of hundreds of train movements involving over a thousand drivers. We were all familiar with progress chasers in workshops. I often thought that either of those titles would have been apt for the job I was now attempting.

As in any similar office job, there were daily phone calls, enquiries and letters. Any week would tell its own story, but a flavour of the work might be glimpsed in this one. It included work in connection with Monktonhall Colliery; preparation for the Wallace Lecture; involvement with the Edinburgh Chamber of Commerce; conversation with Campbell Christie of the STUC; writing to church leaders in Scotland in connection with the Assembly Report; discussion with English industrial mission about their possible involvement with us in the oil industry; discussion at the STUC about a possible joint conference with Industrial Mission; contact from the Australian United Church about industrial mission; discussion with the Church of Scotland press office over an emergency in a church sponsored YTS programme; preparation for a lecture I had been asked to give at the Christian Resources Exhibition; and work in connection with a book we were having published, *New Patterns of Work.*

In order to do the task effectively, I had to keep in touch with a number of key organisations and individuals. I was on the Executive of the Scottish Council Development and Industry; regularly attended the International Forum; was a member of the Scottish Forum for Training Measures; and kept in touch with Church Action on Poverty, Church Action with the Un-employed and a number of other similar bodies linked to economic and social issues. There was a vast amount of reading to get through, some of which arrived in the form of journals and periodicals. These included the *Employment Gazette, Industrial Society, Business Insider, New Economics, Work Research Unit,* the *Journal of Business Ethics,* and others. I main-tained files and cuttings in relation to the issues and industries with which we were involved and forwarded, or kept, these for colleagues.

There never had been a full-time industrial organiser or chaplain for the Edinburgh area and so I decided to develop regular contact with the Chamber of Commerce, the Trades Council, the Trade Union and Community Resource Centre, Napier College, Edinburgh University, the Convention of Scottish Local Authorities, and a range of individuals.

Looking back it might have been wiser for me to forego the basic instincts of a chaplain working at local level, and develop more strongly the links at national level, but I felt I needed a local chaplaincy to keep a balance. I became, therefore, chaplain at Ferranti.

For over forty years, Ferranti had been a major manufacturer and a major employer in the Edinburgh area. There was a long-standing link with indus-trial mission going back to the Revd Ian Reid, minister at the Old Kirk in Pilton. He had been the chaplain at Crewe Toll Works. Every one of his successors – Colin Anderson, Tom Kerr, Ian Moir and Tom Preston – were chaplains there. Ferranti also had other plants in the city and five of us from different denominations were chaplains in these. My predecessor, George Wilkie, had visited the Ferranti drawing offices. I went into the management services headquarters at Bellesk House, as well as a plant at West Shore Road.

I always found these visits rewarding and refreshing and a helpful balancing ingredient to me in the midst of other pressures – whatever good they may otherwise have been to those I met.

During the later years of my association with Ferranti, I ministered in a context all too familiar to me in previous chaplaincies. It was new to Ferranti employees, however. For many years the staff had enjoyed well-paid jobs and a high level of job security largely because they worked in the defence sector. The company had what was called a 'cost plus' relationship with the Government. This was suddenly disturbed by three factors: the take-over of the company by GEC, the resulting new competitive culture, and the threat of major cut-backs throughout the defence sector.

Very rapidly, senior directors and managers, who had been man and boy Ferranti people, left the company. There were major redundancies. Those remaining looked askance at those who were leaving for the last time, and wondered who were the more fortunate – those who knew the worst and were in a position to begin a new life beyond Ferranti, or those remaining. I felt the company was not handling redundancies well. I suggested to Ian Moir, the Crewe Toll chaplain, that we arrange a meeting with senior directors to suggest improvements. We met, some changes were made, but I cannot say we were really successful.

As a result of working with Ferranti, I began to develop, with others, a local arms diversification network which explored alternative uses for the skills and resources within the defence industry.

Reports were also prepared for the Church and Nation Committee of the Church of Scotland; for the Action of Churches Together in Scotland's Commission for Peace, Justice, Social and Moral Issues; and for the IMA's defence network.

New Appointments in Glasgow in the 1980s

My move from Glasgow to the organiser's job based in Edinburgh meant there would be a vacancy for the industrial chaplaincy post in Glasgow. The Glasgow team wished to continue as a planning and operational group, with the mutual support and effective working they already enjoyed. We all hoped for the appointment of someone who would have commitment and enthusiasm for industrial mission, a mix of experience and knowledge, and who would be an asset to the work, both in Glasgow and in Scotland. It was with relief that Norman Orr was appointed. His experience had ideally prepared him for the work. He was a professional graduate engineer whose call to the ministry came later. In his Church Extension parish in Greenock he had worked alongside others in the early experiments in industrial mission. When he became chaplain to the University of Dundee, he was a great supporter of the work of the first full-time industrial chaplain in Dundee, Roger Clarke. After his term as University Chaplain, he went for a number of years to work at Howdens as a design engineer. There he began to explore the possibility of becoming some kind of worker priest. He wanted to persuade both the company and the Home Board of the Church of Scotland to recognise him as a minister in Howdens. He wanted the company to allocate enough time to do the work. He came often to discuss this with me and I supported him. Unfortunately neither the company nor the Home Board seemed willing for this, and although we in industrial mission in Glasgow supported him it was less than he wished. Nevertheless, he developed within Howdens, along with key laymen like Ian McCartney, also on our local industrial committee, a Howdens group of company staff who met weekly to discuss the inter-action of Christian faith and the issues of industrial life. This group made a number of initiatives for the good of the company.

When he was appointed to the full-time industrial mission post in Glasgow, he dreamt of developing similar groups in other companies. To his disap-pointment, he found this was not easy and, in the end, it proved impossible. He had to acknowledge that a chaplain's situation is different from that of an employee. He turned his attention to the development of lay training in what were called the Seafar experiments. This play upon words related to the place where the group met to develop programmes of action for lay people at work (Seafar House in Cumbernauld), and to a vision. Norman also followed me in the chaplaincy initiated at Govan Shipbuilders and became much involved in British maritime policy. He was, I think, less of a team person than the others in the team, and to some extent the strong team activity in Glasgow of previous years withered a bit.

For several years before his retirement, he became interested in the sad closure of British Rail Engineering Limited in Springburn. The local churches had created a group to seek alternative employment. Maxwell Davidson, an Edinburgh consultant engineer, had for many years been attempting to develop a small steam engine which would be of value in Third World countries. Norman joined with him and created a development group employing several men under their direction. Industrial Mission supported the project with funds and Norman had the pleasure, before his untimely death, of knowing that it could succeed.

His death was felt deeply by us all. He had been known in the Church as 'indefatigable' or, sometimes, the champion of lost causes. He was certainly strongly focused on what he believed to be the supremely important things in life, faith and industry, and peace issues. The vacancy created by his retirement had fortunately been filled with the appointment of Angus Turner.

Angus had worked for some years as a missionary teacher in Africa. On his return to Glasgow, he was appointed Associate Minister at Renfield St Stephen's Church, in the centre of the city. Fortunately, he had the vision of seeing that church as an appropriate base for Christian ministry and service to the life of the city. His first attempts to create outward looking groups within the church were not successful. After discussing it with him, we decided to link up and use some of the industrial mission techniques which we had developed in making contact with offices and managements. Increasingly, Angus found the alliance between his city centre work and our wider work of industrial mission to be helpful and mutually supportive. We were delighted when the Board of National Mission of the Church of Scotland, as it now was, appointed him to the Glasgow post.

Angus continued faithfully and effectively as a chaplain in Govan Shipbuilders. The industry had gone through many difficult periods, but during these years the take-over of the company by the Norwegian firm Kvaerner, was to mark a massive change. His advice and experience proved valuable to the company in many ways. Pastoral work with the workers, insights and contributions from him at times of crisis, quiet negotiations in our small Elmbank Street office with both sides during industrial relations problems, and mending of relationships between managers, was the mix of his ministry.

During these years also he built up a strong relationship with Strathclyde Regional Council. A number of us had already developed informal contact with staff members at various levels. Now he and Campbell Robertson, the Community Minister at Anderson Kelvingrove, were appointed chaplains to the Region. They were provided with an office in which to meet individuals and groups. Campbell's early death meant that Angus had to continue this large task on his own. Fortunately, he had already built links with many in the Region before the worst of the fears and anxieties began to affect staff in the run up to the change in local authority structure in 1996.

Learning from Clinical Theology

My own personal growth and maturity in the mid 1970s benefited from meetings with Hamish Montgomery, a tutor in Clinical Theology. Clinical theology, a study of the deep psychological roots of human growth and personality, was developed by Dr Frank Lake. It formed the basis of a Christian pastoral theology.

Once a month for two years, I was one of a dozen people meeting in Hamish's home, where he and his wife Isobel helped us to understand ourselves and each other better. We explored frankly, and sometimes to our embarrassment, the way we were made and what we might become. We looked at the origins of personality and the development of identity through birth, childhood and life. Using group dynamics, and with some practical counselling, we gained a new understanding of care of the aged, parenthood, bereavement, and depression.

Whilst a minister in my first parish, I underwent psychoanalysis and I also shared group psycho-analysis with people in nursing, teaching, ministry and social work. I felt I gained greatly from those experiences. I understood myself better and felt I had become a better pastor. It seemed to improve the quality of my visiting yards and factories. Many like me owe a great debt to Hamish Montgomery and to Frank Lake, who came to our group on several occasions.

During this period Hamish and I also met regularly with Gerald Hely, the hospital chaplain at Gartnaval General, for mutual support. We met at Gartnaval and spent lunch and an hour or so sharing our experiences. Usually each related a pastoral situation with which he was involved. We discussed it and helped each other think it through. I found this of much value.

The Commitment of Local Chaplains

In over fifty years of industrial mission in Scotland, no more than twenty ministers have been appointed full-time chaplains. In that same period well over a thousand ministers have served as part-time or, more accurately, local chaplains. In the midst of parish and/or congregational work, they regularly visit local enterprises. Full-timers, each usually with three or four chaplaincies, are area industrial mission organisers. They have a wide variety of other tasks and responsibilities in relation to ministering to people at work. Local chaplains express industrial mission concerns within enterprises in the same way as full-timers.

As with any group of people, the level of commitment of local chaplains, their enthusiasm and effectiveness varies. I have had the disappointment of negotiating successfully with management and trade unions to allow a chaplain to enter a company, to find after some months that the chaplain has not been visiting. Others have continued for years, winning a place of warm acceptance in the company and with employees. When they moved on, it was my task to try and arrange for a new chaplain. In most cases I was successful.

Local chaplaincy has always been a low profile piece of work. Some congregations have been glad that their minister was engaged in this missionary outreach and supported his task. Others even encouraged the minister to take it up. Some thought their minister was dissipating his energies in directions outwith the needs of the congregation. Some companies simply tolerated the chaplain. In others, after a slow start, there was growing appreciation of the chaplain's contribution to the life of the company.

At the end of World War II, in the days of the 'The Industrial Chaplaincy Scheme', the General Assembly of the Church of Scotland were told there were '230 chaplains with thirty other industrial establishments awaiting appointments'. For a number of reasons this large number has never been repeated. Surprisingly, in spite of the many pressures on ministers and priests, and in spite of the inevitable movement of clergy across the country, there have always been about a hundred active local chaplains.

Many work on their own, motivated solely by their own understanding of ministry and by their conviction that they must work outside the structures of the Church.

In some areas local chaplains regularly meet. Some groups meet monthly for mutual support, sometimes with a full-time chaplain. The Hawick and Borders team is a good example of local chaplains organising themselves: first under the leadership of Colin Forrester-Paton and then under the leadership of Revd Stanley Britton, a local Congregational minister. They also gathered a local Church and Industry Committee. They have held a number of conferences on the textile industry and on the industry's multi-fibre agreement. They have tried to help the unemployed through unemployment open-days, and some members have served on the Borders Business Institute of Management. Annual conferences and occasional training courses are held to assist local chaplains. Speakers from the SCDA, the STUC, the Industrial Society, and the CBI, have shared in these.

In 1989, John Davidson, then director of the Scottish CBI, addressed chaplains in Carronvale House near Larbert, a few weeks before his untimely death. More ambitious two day chaplains courses have been held, and thirty attended a very successful three day course at Stirling University. On occasion, these courses have had the assistance of industrial mission colleagues from England, including Julian Eagle of Hampshire Industrial Mission, Ray Taylor, a Baptist chaplain from South Wales, and Mike West, the leader of the Sheffield Team. It was always a pleasure for me to visit industrial sites with other chaplains and I regret not doing more of this.

With the local chaplain, there is a sense in which I represented the interest of the wider church. It reminded companies that the regular visits of the local chaplain were not solely the result of personal interest, but part of the interest of the wider Church in industry and commerce. On many occasions, the joint visit opened new doors for the chaplain. It also helped me understand better what was going on in other industries. Local chaplains often spoke of the pastoral aspect of their role. One spoke about the personal anxieties and problems of a personnel manager which were adversely affecting the company. Another spoke of a managing director's dictatorial style of which many in the company were complaining. The local chaplain's task was not easy and I often admired their courage.

I remember being in the Rosevale Cinema in Partick with Frank Kennedy. The smoky atmosphere of the bingo hall was the setting for the 10th Anniversary of the Upper Clyde Shipbuilders' struggle. I was underground with Hugh Ormiston, and in ICI's factory in Dumfries with Bill McKenzie. I flew to Dounreay at the request of the managing director of the power station anxious to find a successor to the chaplain who had recently moved. I visited Grangemouth Dock Yard, and introduced a new chaplain to the Edinburgh engineering company, Brown Brothers, having negotiated with Ken Bonnington, the managing director. I visited the Creamery at Stranraer in the south of Scotland, and the Sunchild clothing factory there. I introduced Myra Smith to Gates Rubber Company in Dumfries as the new chaplain, went to the famous machine tool makers, Lewis and Giddons Fraser at Arbroath, with Guy Brownlee their chaplain, and to Webster Textiles, also in Arbroath, with their chaplain Bob Glover.

Andrew Wylie took me to the Off Shore Exhibition in Aberdeen. Later we were to go to the Claymore platform and the rescue ship 'Tharos', following the Piper Alpha disaster. I visited GEC's factory at Kirkcaldy with Bill Lyons and met the manager of Longannet Power Station – Scotland's largest. These were only some of many dozens of site visits made over the years.

CHAPTER 10

Industries
and Mission

THIS brief record cannot possibly give a full account of the traumas which struck sector after sector of Scottish industry in the past two decades. Nor can it adequately describe the ways in which industrial mission responded. Some at least must be mentioned.

The Shipbuilding Industry –
the Cradle of Industrial Mission in Scotland

The cradle of industrial mission in Scotland was the shipbuilding industry and we are still working work with it. Even before George Wilkie's appointment to the yards, there were parish ministers working in them as local chaplains. The first full-time industrial chaplain in Scotland, Cameron Wallace, was appointed to the yards of the lower reaches of the Clyde. He gained wide respect for the Church during his ministry there at all levels. During periods of industrial unrest, Cameron quietly moved between the parties gaining the confidence of both management and shop stewards.

In the early 1960s, George Wilkie, while National Organiser, arranged discussions with workers and managers concerned with shipbuilding at Fairfield in Govan.

From the beginning of my own appointment, I was in touch with the same industry. Though I had chaplaincies in engineering companies, it will be remembered that Frank Kennedy and I operated a joint chaplaincy in the yards of the upper Clyde.

When Cameron moved to a parish, Colin Anderson was appointed to the Lower Reaches. This brought to the industry a man of dedication whose work is still warmly remembered and appreciated. Shortly after Colin's appointment, there was growing concern for the future of the industry. With the co-operation of the Glasgow team, we decided to hold a 'hearing' on shipbuilding. We studied many reports on the industry and read widely the

Parliamentary documents on the subject. A number of people selected for their knowledge of the industry were invited to meet us to respond to our questions.

There were particular types of people we wanted to hear from – ship-building directors, trade unionists, groups of workers and managers in the industry, ship-owning and ship-managing directors, economists, academics, and politicians. In all 45 people were interviewed during the course of the two week consultation period. Our report was well received by the industry, and two years later we were still receiving comments from organisations related to the industry.

When Colin was appointed to the Lower Reaches, 11,000 people were employed directly in the shipbuilding industry, and, indirectly, three times as many. There were nine yards and three engineering works on the lower reaches, five yards on the upper Clyde and smaller yards in Leith, Dundee and Aberdeen. All were to face a period of great change. A corporate plan had been devised for the nationalised shipbuilding industry: Upper Clyde Ship-builders in Govan would tender for merchant ships, with the lower reaches focusing on naval and oil-related work. But there was no Government support, not even in terms of an overall policy for the industry, and danger began to threaten.

When I left Glasgow in 1980 to become National Organiser, Norman Orr continued the chaplaincy at Govan. Soon after he was in post, British Shipbuilders urged employees to accept a 'Survival Plan' under which half the workforce on the lower reaches of the Clyde would lose their jobs. The crisis came at the end of 1982 when, two weeks before Christmas, a major contract for Britoil was cancelled. Industrial mission took a keen interest. I contacted the chief executive of British Shipbuilders at his home in Canada. The Church and Industry Committee in Greenock Presbytery was approached by British Shipbuilders who, wrongly as it turned out, thought the Committee had approved of the Survival Plan. Greenock commissioners to the 1983 General Assembly asked the Assembly to support the workers in their struggle to maintain jobs. This it did and afterwards the Moderator met the shop stewards and later visited the yard.

The development of Church support, encouraged by Colin and the local Church and Industry Committee Convener, Ian Black, was to prove important. A 'World in Action' television programme of January 1984 drew heavily on the Church's involvement. Mrs Thatcher, then Prime Minister, received a deputation led by Jimmy Milne of the General Secretary of the STUC, and soon after, with her encouragement, Trafalgar House bought the yards on the lower reaches.

Colin's contribution to industrial mission has been widely recognised.

He continued in the area as a parish minister and Regional Councillor before becoming Chaplain to the University of Glasgow. The credibility of industrial mission in the area rests on the fact that he and the local Church and Industry Committee took the issues seriously, did not jump to conclusions or endorse everything, but stuck responsibly to their role.

The Scottish team had already met several times with British Shipbuilders' directors, both at their headquarters in Newcastle and in London. Later we developed a shipbuilding chaplains' network across the United Kingdom, and Alister Goss, the present full-time chaplain in Greenock, Norman Orr and Brian Hailes of Northumberland Industrial Mission, organised a very effective maritime policy conference in London in 1987.

The Long Association with the Steel Industry

Industrial mission has also had a long association with the steel industry. Peter Houston was one of a number of local chaplains working in the industry when it was still in the private sector. They developed works visiting and provided training programmes for apprentices. In 1966 Sandy Ryrie, who had served as a Church of Scotland missionary in India, was appointed the first full time chaplain in North Lanarkshire. The steel industry was soon be nationalised and Sandy was quickly caught up in a time of exciting change. This appointment was a significant one for industrial mission, since the industry dominated much of the West of Scotland.

Sandy began by working alongside workers on various shifts and soon became widely accepted as an integral part of the life of the industry. He established a number of study groups and produced, as a result of the discussions, a number of valuable short papers linking faith, work and the responsibility of Christians.

Sandy was one of the most able industrial chaplains we have had working with us. His commitment to the industry, and his ability to analyse human and industrial situations and imbue them with thoughtful insights from the Gospel and Christian theology, combined to make him, as I thought, the ideal future leader of industrial mission in Scotland. We all greatly felt his loss when, following an illness, he decided to leave industrial mission. He continued to contribute ably to Scottish education and, more recently, to the work of the Scottish Episcopal Church.

The vacant post of Industrial Chaplain in North Lanarkshire was filled by the Home Board of the Church of Scotland with the appointment of John Potter, a Methodist minister in Glasgow. This also underlined the ecumenical nature of the work. Some time earlier I had persuaded the Director of the

Methodist Industrial Mission College at Luton to find a Methodist minister
with some experience of Industrial Mission to come and work in the Glasgow
Methodist circuit and share in industrial mission. The Revd John Potter and
his wife and young family were willing to make the move to Glasgow, Maryhill. He had worked with industrial mission in Coventry and had readily
engaged in industrial mission in Glasgow. He was to serve the industry very
ably for the next twenty years until the steelworks at Ravenscraig closed.

He gave an excellent insight into the industry in his report, 'The Steel
Industry through the eyes of Church and Industry', in which he wrote:

> *The steel industry was in private hands after the war and was then
> nationalised by the Labour Government, privatised by the Conservatives,
> and again nationalised by Labour in 1967. It is a highly political indus-
> try which generates a great deal of wealth for the local community. It
> needs significant amounts of investment from time to time to keep it live
> and well and competitive.*
>
> **Steel closures are not new.**
>
> *In 1973 the Heath Government announced a £3 billion investment
> programme for the industry in Britain.* [In today's values that would be
> approaching £30 billion.] *Lord Melchett was the chairman and Monty
> Finniestone chief executive, but there was a price to be paid in terms of
> the closure of all the open hearth facilities and many of the older mills.
> When the Labour Government came into power, the Beswick committee
> decided that there should be a two year notice of closure.*
>
> *Church and Industry was involved in training courses for redundancy
> counsellors. The survival kit was widely used and there was a great deal
> of informal counselling discussions with individuals and groups, of the
> move. The British Steel Corporation (BSC) had a sophisticated social
> policy headed up by Ron Smith who moved from the post of general
> secretary of the Post Workers' Union to be the director of social policy.
> It was the age of consultation and industrial democracy and the BSC
> invited local communities to respond to the plans for change. I was
> invited to serve on the local Motherwell and Wishaw Burgh Committee
> and in the end we produced a report entitled 'Steel, and the Implications
> of Change'. This resulted in a letter from the BSC local management at
> Ravenscraig questioning my role on the committee. The unions in the
> plant were also concerned about my identification with the older works.
> I replied that I was serving on the committee at the invitation of the
> Council and that we were responding to BSC's invitation to analyse the
> impact on the local economy and the people .*
>
> *There was the inevitable protest train to London and local demon-*

evd William McIntyre

'd Cameron Wallace (right)

Revd Ted Wickham

Revd George Wilkie

Revd Sandy Ryrie (right)

evd Roger Clarke

Revd John Potter

evd Colin Anderson

Father Frank Kennedy

Revd Dr Hugh Ormiston

Revd Andrew Wylie

(Left to right, back row) Donald Rennie, Bill Anderson, Fred Darwent – (Front row) Donald Ross, Andrew Wylie

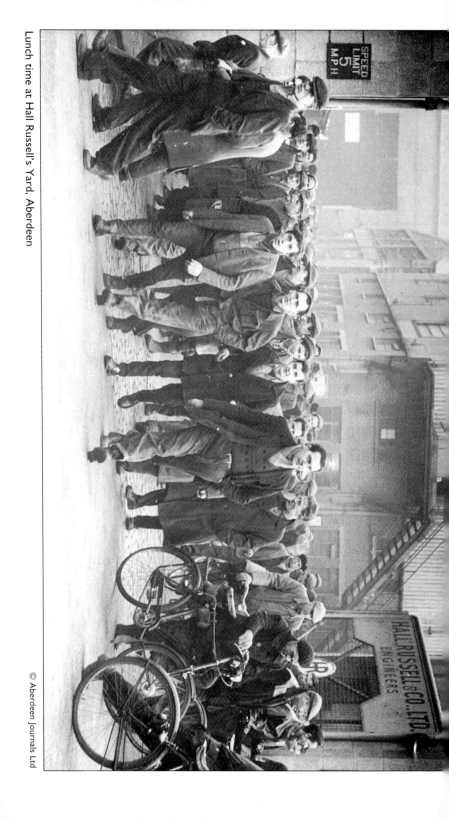

Lunch time at Hall Russell's Yard, Aberdeen

© Aberdeen Journals Ltd

(left to right) Revd John Potter, Revd Erik Cramb, Revd Angus Smith,
Revd Dr Hugh Ormiston and Revd Bill Rayne

Revd Donald Ross

strations. We managed to persuade the local churches to come out onto the streets to share in the expression of concern with the assurance that there would be no political banners. Then on the day in question, just as the march was due to set off, up went the Scottish National Party flags and trouble broke out!

Many of the action committee were frustrated by the response of members in the working situation who were not prepared to take a longer view of the scene and who voted to take redundancy payments bringing about the permanent closure of a number of facilities.

At the same time, new investment was earmarked for Ravenscraig in iron and steel-making, in opencast as well as in the new ore terminal at Hunterston. The opening of Hunterston marked the high point of investment, but even that event was overshadowed by the dispute with the dockers which threatened the future of Ravenscraig itself.

The steel strike of 1980 was a turning point indeed, and during the long weeks of the strike I was involved in meetings and pastoral support and court appearances It was the first major strike during the Thatcher years with lessons for everyone. During these turbulent times, relationships and understandings were strengthened and provided the foundation for the next phase.

After the strike the threat of closure was very real. The Ravenscraig plant had not had time to prove itself and survival plans and local lump sum bonuses came into fashion putting local lay officials under enormous pressure. I am sure that the decision to close Ravenscraig was made in 1982, but it was frustrated by responsible lobbying and better plant performance. The lay officials developed new ways of relating to the wider world.

I was involved in much of the work behind the scenes and in setting up meetings with various public bodies. The shop stewards insisted that I should accompany them on their visits and so began a series of meetings with Government ministers and political leaders. The stewards decided that the days of demonstration were over and that thorough preparation and documentation and discipline were important in the lobbying process. Traditional trade unionists had been dependent on noisy demonstrations and verbal blasts.

I well remember meeting with George Younger, then Secretary of State for Scotland. It was held in Whitehall and, after a constructive meeting, we came out to face the press. The instinct of some of the full-time official was to slam the Government. That was what was expected. We told them in no uncertain terms that this was not now the name of the game, and that that door would never open again.

I encouraged them to go and seek out strange bedfellows in the search for support and I shall never forget the look on the face of the Conservative party official in Edinburgh as our delegation made its way in to see Michael Ancrum who was then the chairman of the Conservative party in Scotland.

They also met Church leaders in Edinburgh and increasingly the Church of Scotland's Church and Nation Committee was drawn into the debate.

I also recall yet another meeting in Edinburgh with the Secretary of State for Scotland. The meeting lasted a full hour. Afterwards I apologised for not making a contribution. The stewards rounded on me, 'Your presence and help in the preparation and evaluating afterwards are vital'. I was put in my place.

The 1984 miners' strike was a painful chapter. Many of the activists in the labour movement wanted the steel works to shut down in support of the miners. If that had happened the plant would never have opened again. In industrial mission this caused some real problems, with Hugh Ormiston [a chaplain with the mining industry since 1980] *in strong support of the miners and yours truly in equally strong support of the steel workers. There was a high public profile through those days and always the danger that BSC would say enough is enough, and keep the chaplain at bay. Although I did try to ensure that I would not indulge in easy public criticism of BSC since it would not help the cause.*

So much happened that it is difficult to condense it into a few paragraphs, but I still value most of all the quiet work behind the scenes with people at every level in the industry, trying to lend support and encouragement to people at work. In the end the plant closed.

British Steel got its way as part of the price of privatisation. So what was the use of all that campaigning? I remember the initial planning stage when it was obvious that the works was at risk. The decision was made that when that day of closure came it would not be possible to point the finger at the poor performance of the works and use that as an excuse for closure. That objective was achieved and most of the people in the plant were able to leave with their heads held high, with justifiable pride in performance and, at senior level in the trade unions, a sense of achievement. They had not prevented the closure of the plant, but they had delayed it for a significant length of time. They had also developed new ways of working as trade unions which could provide a model for others.

What of industrial mission in all this? It is difficult to pass a verdict on something you were yourself so intimately involved in. It was however an enormous privilege to be able to stand together with people at work passing through such demanding times. The long haul pays dividends No one could doubt our commitment to the people and the industry. At key moments we were able to shape and influence events. Others of us were involved in other ways in the changing fortunes of the steel industry since it affected so much of Scotland's industrial life.

For John, however, the closure of Ravenscraig was a personal loss. His ministry had been so bound up with it that the transition for him to other aspects of the work was difficult. But industry continued and ministry continued, and many people are grateful for his mission and service among them.

The Development of the Work on Tayside

We always tried to provide an effective industrial mission presence within each of Scotland's major industrial areas. This aim was more fully realised when Roger Clarke, the Church of Scotland minister at Stepps, was appointed full-time chaplain in Dundee in February 1972. Roger had taught science for a number of years before becoming a parish minister. As in other areas of Scotland, the dominant industries, large employers of labour, were undergoing change. The city of Jute, Jam and Journalism was no longer depending on these industries.

New engineering plants, a growth in food distribution and new industrial estates were providing employment, while unemployment was dramatically on the increase. While industrial mission was trying to respond to the situation, Roger was particularly concerned about unemployment. He set up a lot of practical schemes which helped very many people, and with his gift for stimulating writing he constantly raised the issues around unemployment. His book, *Work in Crisis – Dilemma of a Nation*, was published in 1982.

In it he described the effects of the loss of the ideal of employment. A two nation society was being created where some, with a regular job, lived in comparative affluence, while others were in danger of forming an unemployed underclass. He explored the significance of work and the social isolation of the unemployed. He alleged the old work ethic was anachronistic and wrestled with the problem of sharing opportunities for work. He called for new attitudes to affirm the value of the unemployed and the creation of what he called a 'contribution ethic'.

Tragically the two nation state is still with us. The challenge of adapting lifestyles in a world of high levels of unemployment remains. Roger made a significant contribution to industrial mission and to the market of ideas around the world of work. His gifts were recognised when he was appointed Joint Director of the William Temple Foundation – a think-tank for industrial mission and similar work based in Manchester.

In January 1985, Roger was succeeded by John Ross. John was an Australian who had served as a chaplain in the Australian Navy. A member of the Iona Community, he worked in Govan, and later at the World Council of Churches in Italy where he became fluent in Italian. On his return to Scotland he had a most effective ministry at Battlefield in Glasgow before being appointed an industrial chaplain.

Though Australian, his many friends would agree that the Scot's phrase 'bonnie fechter' could well describe him. He was strongly of the mind that Christian mission must take place in the secular and political arenas. However, his chaplaincy in Dundee was short.

The Board of World Mission and Unity of the Church of Scotland, recognising the value of his experience in Italy, called him to the Scot's Kirk in Rome. There he took seriously ill, was brought back to Glasgow where he died shortly thereafter to the great loss of all who knew him.

Erik Cramb succeeded him in Dundee in 1989 after good ministries in Dalmarnock, Glasgow, Kingston, Jamaica and again in Glasgow, at Yoker. In each of his ministries he had strongly identified with the powerless and the exploited. As the son of a Glasgow shipyard worker, he knew the background of working life. As one who is himself physically handicapped, he knows the problems of people with disabilities. His own handicap he overcomes daily to the point where people simply do not see it because of the dynamism within him.

Erik began what he called his 'industrial wanderings' by making contact with people at all levels in Dundee. He made a point of visiting the local ministers to develop friendships and foster understanding of industrial mission.

The years in Tayside have been turbulent. One large industrial concern and three smaller companies were formed by buy-outs from the original National Cash Register company. One of these became, for over a year, the locus of one of the most bitter industrial lock-outs of recent years. The sheer injustice of the situation ensured Erik's daily support for all affected. This was still rumbling on when the Timex lock-out began. Again Erik was in daily support, calling for the wider support of the Church.

Forth Valley acquires a Full-time Chaplain

In the mid 1970s, with the agreement of the Church of Scotland's Home

Board and the Church and Industry Committee, George Wilkie arranged a number of meetings with the relevant committees of the Presbytery of Kilmarnock and the Presbytery of Falkirk. There was Church support in both of those areas for the appointment of a full-time industrial chaplain. Industrial development seemed more clearly evident, at that time, in the Grangemouth and Forth Valley area. While the coal industry remained in the area, it was dominated by a huge and growing chemical industry. A busy port and a variety of other industries, from coach-building and garment manufacture to bookbinding, were also in the area.

To the disappointment of Kilmarnock, the post of full-time chaplain was advertised for the Forth Valley. Without doubt the appointment of Hugh Ormiston was one of the significant factors for the success of industrial mission in the years following and till now. Hugh's experience and abilities were made for industrial mission.

His engineering apprenticeship with the North British Locomotive Company in Springburn and at Polmadie in Glasgow, following a short period at sea with the Anchor Line, gave him a solid base. Though not from a religious or church-going family, he committed himself to Christ in the late 1950s and was one of the many young people influenced by the ministry of Tom Allan at St George's Tron church in Glasgow. As with Cameron Wallace, George Wilkie, Norman Orr and myself, he invested an early part of his ministry in Church Extension: in his case, the difficult parish of Whitfield in Dundee.

In addition to his practical experience, Hugh's intellectual gifts were to prove an enormous asset. He could analyse, write and present perspectives on industrial matters which were discussed with vigour, if not always agreed to, by the rest of us in the team. His research into the influence of Japanese industry on United Kingdom companies was especially valuable. The fruits of that work were fed, practically and intellectually, into the life of the team and of industrial mission in Scotland.

At the time of his appointment it seemed wise to Industrial Mission that work should begin with what was then the National Coal Board (NCB) and the mining community in the Forth Valley. This would not be easy, since access to men underground needed specialised training and particular arrangements, for safety reasons. The NCB trained Hugh, together with a local Roman Catholic priest, Father Charles Henry, at Comrie colliery, and underground visits began at the large Longannet mining complex on the north bank of the Forth. Fortunately roots had time to develop before the 1984-85 miners' strike which dominated British industrial relations for several years.

The Miners' Strike in Scotland tests Industrial Mission

The 1984 miners' strike was one of the most significant industrial disputes of the past twenty years. The banning of trade union membership at the Government's GCHQ led the President of the National Union of Mineworkers (NUM), Arthur Scargill, to believe there was a strong possibility that public sympathy could be raised, not only against pit closures, but in preserving mining communities and the balance of working class power in Britain.

The miners in Scotland began their strike in early March 1984. Hugh had already built good relationships with both management and miners and had learned much of the problems, dangers, industrial relations and economic factors of the industry. When the dispute began, he continued visiting miners wherever they could be found, mainly in strike centres and on picket duty, and expressed general sympathy for the position of the NUM. Wisely, he retained contacts with management. As the dispute continued, public debate raged throughout Scotland. Tensions developed between the steel workers at Ravenscraig, who wished to maintain full production to preserve their own jobs, and the NUM who wanted to disrupt coal to the steelworks to assist their own case.

By mid-summer it looked as though the strike would last until the autumn of 1984. Already hardship was being experienced in mining communities and the women began to organise soup kitchens. Some employers allowed funds to be collected from their employees and most trade unionists gave considerable support. In May of that same year the General Assembly of the Church of Scotland encouraged congregations to provide food for local strike centres and this did happen to some extent.

The dispute is a matter of public record. Newspapers, radio and TV bulletins constantly reported upon the noisy altercations during picketing, the dangerous speed of lorries trying to enter premises, the tactics of the police and the miners' leaders, and discussions about the prospects of success or otherwise for the miners or the Government. Inevitably, Hugh Ormiston was involved daily.

The miners took heart from his constant presence, and while much of the public turned increasingly against the miners, he, industrial mission, and many churches, continued to understand and support them in their plight.

With representatives of the Church of Scotland's Church and Nation Committee, Hugh and I went to the NCB headquarters in Edinburgh to meet the Scottish Director, Albert Wheeler, who was annoyed at the General Assembly's decision to help the families of miners. We also met Mick McGahey, George Bolton and Erik Clarke, the Scottish miners' leaders, at the NUM headquarters, also in Edinburgh. They insisted that the NCB's concern was short-term, while their concern lay with the long-term interest of the industry.

In the middle of July, myself, on behalf of industrial mission, Maxwell Craig representing the Church and Nation Committee, and Father Jim McShane of the Scottish Catholic Justice and Peace Commission, wrote to Mrs Thatcher with copies to other Government ministers, to the NCB, and to Arthur Scargill, urging Mrs Thatcher to bring both sides together. After discussions with us, the Moderator of the Church of Scotland General Assembly, Jim Paterson, stated formally that, 'Mrs Thatcher should make every effort to bring the two sides together with a view to talks recommencing'. When he and I visited the Presbytery of Fife, he remarked on the weakness of local church contact with the mining industry.

In St Giles Cathedral, the evening before the huge '84 Miners' Gala Day in Edinburgh, we held a prayer vigil attended by Bruce Kent, the leader of the peace movement, and a speaker at the Gala the next day. Hugh shared the platform with him at the Gala, when around forty thousand people attended.

In November Hugh and his colleague chaplains in the coal network met with Ian McGregor, the NCB chairman, at the industry's head office, Hobart House in London.

By November there was a drift back to work and, in the following January, a growing conviction that the miners' action was lost and that many mining families and communities faced the permanent loss of jobs and extreme financial difficulty. In May 1985 we reported to the Church and Industry Committee on our meetings with the new management team of the NCB and that we had arranged meetings between the new Assembly Moderator, Bob Craig, and the new Director of the NCB in Scotland, George McAlpine, followed by a meeting with the unchanged Scottish NUM leadership.

Shortly after the dispute, the Centre for Theology and Public Issues at the University of Edinburgh held a conference called 'The Scottish Churches and the Political Process Today'. The following is the brief contribution I made at the time on our involvement with the mining dispute and some of the lessons derived from it.

The Churches' Response to the Miners' Strike

The miners' strike is an important case study of the Church's role in industrial and political disputes, not least because there was much less agreement within the churches than had been the case at times of industrial unrest in steel, shipbuilding and vehicle manufacture. This will not be the last controversial problem in our rapidly changing society, so it is important that we learn through whom the Church should speak, and when, and how to do so with most effect.

There are various ways in which the Church can speak on industrial and political matters. It has a symbolic voice. Many of us have been on public marches to indicate that the churches include many with strong theologically rooted feelings about economic and political issues. Even when this does not carry the full weight of church opinion, it is important. I believe this symbolic presence was well demonstrated by industrial chaplain Hugh Ormiston during the coal dispute. Not everyone in the churches agreed with him, but it was right that through him a voice was heard reflecting Christian concern.

The Church can also speak through reports and public announcements. The annual reports of the Church and Nation Committee of the Church of Scotland and other church committees exemplify this, as do the written responses produced for consultative documents and green papers. These have included comments on shipbuilding, transport, steel, MSC programmes, trade union legislation, social security, abortion, housing, and many others. The crucial question is how and through whom the churches should speak at the height of a major public debate.

There have recently been two main pressures on the Church of Scotland with regard to speaking out at a time of public tension. The first is that there are now many groups actively seeking support from the churches. Secondly, the media needs a Church spokesperson, but despite decades of ecumenical activity, the churches remain divided. A common spokesperson does not exist.

Different churches have their different mechanisms through which they speak. The Episcopal system seems, on the face of it, to be the simplest in that a bishop can speak on behalf of that church. On local matters, a Church of Scotland presbytery can give a Church of Scotland view. On wider matters, the General Assembly is the appropriate body.

It is easy for a committee convener to abuse the system and go further than warranted, and it is possible for a Moderator's personal view to be confused with the decision of Assembly.

During industrial unrest in the steel, shipbuilding and coal industries, a pattern developed which formed at least a provisional means of avoiding confusion when speaking for the churches in Scotland. A network of hot-lines was developed linking the Church and Nation Committee convener, the appropriate bishop of the Roman Catholic Church, the chairperson of the Roman Catholic Justice and Peace Commission, the Primus of the Episcopal Church, the Secretary of the National Church and

*Industry Committee, and, where one existed, the industrial chaplain to
the industry. In addition, there were links with appropriate opposite
numbers in the denominations in England and Wales*

Differences and Tensions – the Example of the Miners' Strike

In the miners' dispute, Church opinion was divided in much the same way as
opinion was divided in the rest of the community. After Church statements
were made, or following published articles, letters were received and callers
came to church offices, expressing criticism of what had been said. Many were
unsympathetic towards the miners and felt much more should have been
said about violence and victimisation.

But violence and victimisation was condoned, although more sympathy
for the miners' cause was shown than was being voiced by many other com-
mentators. Those in the churches who were most involved with the dispute
were aware that aspects of the miners' case were not being understood.
Prominence was being given to violence and personalities, and not enough
recognition to the prolonged sacrifice of the miners' own material conditions
and their vision of the future.

The role of the Church came into highest public prominence following
David Jenkins' sermon in Durham Cathedral. In Scotland this was followed by
a carefully phrased, ecumenically-agreed statement issued jointly by the
Moderator of the Church of Scotland, Church and Nation Convener, and
Primus of the Episcopal Church in Scotland. (The Roman Catholic Archbishop
did not wish to sign the statement.) It said: 'The Gospel calls us to a ministry
of reconciliation. The Bishop of Durham has a duty to share in this ministry
and we support the main thrust of his sermon in Durham Cathedral last week.'

All agreed there should be a negotiated settlement to the strike. As time
ran out for this, Church statements became a little more prescriptive. How
were these proposals arrived at and were they wise? Was the proposed cool-
ing off period a useful suggestion? Perhaps not. Should closer links have
been forged with the police who played a crucial role in the dispute? Ought
the churches to have remained silent and confined themselves to praying
about the situation? Would it have been better to encourage local response
from presbyteries and dioceses? With major structural differences between
Presbyterian and Episcopal churches in Scotland, is it realistic to expect a
common view of rapidly changing events?

As already stated, a network of contacts linking the major British denominations came into existence out of sheer necessity. Is something more
organised and formal required for future crises? What we can say is that we

were fortunate in this dispute, as in others, having key field staff in close touch with the people most involved and with a good knowledge of the issues. They may have been in danger of being indoctrinated by one side or another to the detriment of their own best judgement, but this is always a risk worth taking. Also, it has to be said, throughout this dispute the Church of Scotland was exceptionally well served by its Press Department.

New Opportunities in the Oil Industry

By the mid 1980s the oil industry in the north east of Scotland was a key factor in the economics of the United Kingdom and was a dominant industrial giant, not only in Aberdeen and the north east, but in the whole of Scotland. Although the Society Religion Technology Project of the Church of Scotland had produced outstanding reports on the industry, like *Scotland's Pipe Dream* and *Turmoil in Scotland*, the offshore industry remained untouched by industrial mission.

There were a number of local chaplains in Aberdeen, but not in the burgeoning oil industry. In the full-time team we believed we should press the Church of Scotland, through its Home Board, to recognise the need. I was therefore asked to prepare a paper making a case for a chaplain. There were 67,000 people working in the industry. Two hundred rigs and platforms were in place, where men and some women lived in dangerous and hazardous conditions. The Home Board agreed to fund a pilot project to gauge the industry's response to an approach from industrial mission.

We knew there were some difficulties. Helicopter and offshore accommodation would be expensive. The demands of chaplaincy in the North Sea amongst many operating companies and many contractors would be remarkably different from previous experience.

In 1986 Andrew Wylie succeeded Colin Anderson as chaplain on the lower reaches of the Clyde. Before this he had had wide experience of parish ministry, a spell as the director of the Scottish Churches Council, several years as minister at the Church of Scotland in Lausanne and, latterly, minister in the Edinburgh city centre charge of St Andrews and St George's. He volunteered to undertake the Home Board's pilot survey.

Though there were initially reservations in the industry, he succeeded in a remarkably short time to open many doors, and it was he who was appointed the first industrial chaplain to the oil industry and to the north east of Scotland. Such was the size of the industry, it virtually absorbed all Andrew's time and it was impossible adequately to develop industrial mission elsewhere in the north east.

The oil industry made it clear from the beginning that it would prefer to fund the chaplaincy itself. Since all other chaplaincies, and the expenses of industrial mission, had until now been provided by the churches, we had reservations about this. Chaplains appointed and paid for by the Church are independent of both trade unions and companies. It was unknown territory for us to have a chaplain paid by a company. A compromise was arrived at whereby Andrew's stipend would be met by the United Kingdom Offshore Operators Association (UKOOA), sent to the Church of Scotland, and then paid as a chaplain in the usual way.

A new trust was set up to oversee the work, to handle his additional expenses and to arrange office accommodation and secretarial assistance. Andrew began an exhausting round of off-shore visits in September 1986. He was soon widely accepted. His urbane manner and wealth of experience dealing with people soon won him a place of trust and confidence within the industry.

All too soon he was immersed in the tragic aftermath of major accidents. The Bristow Helicopter (Chinook) crash and the Piper Alpha disaster threw him into the full glare of the media. His annual reports and occasional papers, 'Reflections and Lessons for the Caring Professions after Piper Alpha' and 'The Church and Incidents', were greatly appreciated. His addresses to presbyteries, church groups, and at major industrial occasions in Aberdeen and London were also appreciated. His views were often sought by Government ministers and senior people in the oil industry.

North East Area Full-time Industrial Mission Organiser

UKOOA's financial underwriting of the oil chaplaincy made it possible to appoint an area Industrial Mission organiser for the north east of Scotland. Donald Rennie, who had for twenty years carried the flag of industrial mission in the north east as chaplain to North Eastern Farmers Ltd (a farmer-owned Agricultural Co-operative) and other enterprises, as well as being the popular parish minister at Cults East parish church, was appointed. He threw himself into the work for the following five years until his retiral, building up a large network of local chaplains and commenting intelligently on a variety of industrial situations.

When Andrew Wylie retired, Angus Smith, formerly Senior Army Chaplain in Scotland, was appointed to the oil chaplaincy. His Hebridean demeanour and gifts of pastoral care still work for the benefit of those in the industry. He previously served in many theatres of military activity, including the Falklands, was entirely familiar with the rigours of helicopter travel, and brief stays in strange surroundings, so that he takes working off-shore in his stride. His continuing ministry amidst the hazards of the North Sea is much appreciated by the industry, although, as with most ministers, he does not always please everybody. He was supported by industrial mission and by the majority in the oil industry, when he refused to hold an annual service of remembrance for those who lost their lives on Piper Alpha. Instead, an annual service of remembrance for all who have lost their lives in the North Sea is held in Aberdeen.

The Fishing Industry

Because of the limited resources of Industrial Mission, it has neglected the fishing industry. Furthermore, a number of other organisations have historically attended to its needs, particularly the British Sailors' Society and the Royal National Mission to Deep Sea Fishermen. These organisations continue to give good pastoral care, and to provide overnight accommodation and food, as well as presenting the Christian Gospel. They are less concerned with the industry's problems, problems which often also affect fishing communities.

From 1986 onwards I developed a slightly closer link with the industry. Visits to key people took place at Peterhead and Fraserburgh, with visits also to the Ministry of Agriculture and Fisheries, the Fishery Protection Service, and the Sea Fish Authority. The Church and Nation Committee of the Church of Scotland began to study the industry and report on its activities.

In August 1986 I made an interesting short voyage on the Fishery Protection vessel 'Westra' on its normal patrol up the east coast of Scotland and learned much about the responsibilities of the crew. To my delight, the captain allowed me to leave the vessel in a twenty foot swell. We had to jump on to a rubber power boat controlled by the ship's seamen. They took me and the officer-of-the-watch across to a number of fishing boats which we boarded. As their nets were being inspected, I began to recognise the needle in the haystack problems of the Fishery Protection Service! Although this visit preceded much of the heated debate about fishing policy in subsequent years, it gave me an introduction to quotas, total allowable catches and the different ways in which fishing interests often compete with each other.

PART 2

The
TASK and ROLE
of
INDUSTRIAL
MISSION

CHAPTER 11

Influencing
the Influencers

IN industrial mission we knew we were powerless during the massive sea changes taking place in the world of work. These changes affected the lives, health, hopes and future of so many of our people. We did what little we could. We must have attended hundreds of meetings in many different companies; we marched, wrote, prepared papers for groups, and petitioned the Government. We made specific recommendations about the benefits system, about the pay of young workers, the long-term unemployed, about many other issues. We worked on the STUC's Standing Commissions on Unemployment, participated in the Government's Special Programmes, addressed rallies, and did everything we thought was useful. Although much of it then was so urgent for us and filled both our days and our diaries, it is lost now in the mists of time, and here I can record only a little of what I remember.

We arranged on two separate occasions a Special Forum on Unemployment Initiatives. These were held in Glasgow at Anderston Kelvingrove Church where we encouraged Church people from all over Scotland to share the ideas and projects they were developing. From this we produced the document 'Some Practical Responses of the Church in a Time of Unemployment', which listed over fifty projects, and was designed to encourage others. Colin Anderson chaired a group in Glasgow which published *Work, Unemployment and Christian Faith*.

At a meeting of the Churches' Industrial Council, Ken Atkinson, then director of the MSC in Scotland, joined John Pollock, the President of the STUC to consider the mis-match between job opportunities and job seekers. On Tayside, Roger Clarke opened the Resource Centre for the Unemployed which was widely regarded as a model and well used for many years. In Edinburgh, Paisley, Glasgow, Greenock and other Presbyteries, we initiated or participated in working parties which encouraged churches to undertake projects.

Industrial mission during those hectic years also produced a book which ran into four separate re-issues – *Redundant? A Personal Survival Kit.* It contained six short chapters headed, 'It could happen to You', 'Redundancy – The Three Stages', 'You are told You will lose your Job', 'While Working your Notice', 'Your Job finishes', 'Psychological Effects of Redundancy', 'Registration and First Steps', 'Job Hunting is a Full-time Business', 'Applying for Jobs' and 'Surviving'. Advice was given to those about to be made redundant. The booklet was widely used and followed by a smaller leaflet, *Lost Your Job? There is Life after Redundancy*, which listed ten steps suggesting what to do in the event of being made redundant.

The RISK project, described earlier in this book, emerged at this time. It provided courses, in company time, before redundancy. It helped thousands, but we were unsuccessful in our attempts to make this normative throughout industry.

We supported the appeal by the Iona Community to the General Assembly of the Church of Scotland for the appointment of someone to specialise in the field of unemployment. John Harvey, then Leader of the Community, and I, both addressed the Assembly and we almost succeeded. But the appeal failed by a few votes.

The Iona Community managed to find enough money to make a three year appointment and Walter Fyfe was appointed. He had worked for a short time as a parish minister in Scotland and also in East Harlem, New York, and with the Gorbals Group. He had also been a labourer and a trade union official. During this three year period, he strongly supported the Credit Union Movement as a practical means of assisting people who were unemployed.

In Fife, George Wilkie, now a parish minister in Kirkcaldy, and a colleague, John Sim, developed a Life and Social Skills programme which was made available to training organisations. In Edinburgh, during the struggle to prevent the closure of a factory employing a large workforce, I drew together a group of ministers and priests which produced an excellent report on unemployment, written up by a very able Catholic priest. As mentioned earlier, industrial mission was heavily involved in local MSC projects and in the broader discussions about the scope and regulation of the various MSC schemes.

The last twenty years saw some of the most dramatic changes in the world of work. Technological, market and political changes drastically altered the structure of work organisation. Government and industrial leaders talked of the need to create slimmed-down companies to compete with the rest of the world. This slimming down, however, was at the expense of hundreds of thousands and finally millions of people's jobs. They were excluded from work.

For all human beings, work is important, and the loss of it for so many experienced people was devastating. Such loss affected mind, body and spirit, marriage and family, hopes and futures, personal respect, identity, dignity and everything else about a human being that is important.

Work is far more than the business of earning a living and has at least five ingredients. It imposes a time structure on the day. It ensures contact and shared experience with people outside the immediate family. It points out goals and purposes beyond the scope of the individual.

It imposes a status of position in life, and gives identity to individuals. It makes people active and gives them a place in the activity of living. When excluded, people realise how important it is for personal identity. We place a value on our work and on other people's estimation of us at work. It relates to questions like: *Who am I? What am I? What have I been? What shall I become? What sort of people accept me? To what group do I belong? To what group will I belong in the next two years – or five – or ten?* We commit ourselves, in various ways, to a self-image which develops from where we are in our working lives. Anything which affects that is highly disturbing. When any unwelcome change is forced upon us, it can even involve a risk to health and mental stability.

To put it in a more commercial way, an entry into an occupation sets an investment going. If we do not follow it through the investment is lost. Neither is that investment always transferable. When we were young we studied, or learned a trade, and we obtained qualifications. As we continued in a particular occupation we learned its language and ethos. As time went on we committed ourselves even more. Each year, every step, every specialisation, added to that investment. Simultaneously, alternatives were closed off.

It is very important to understand the difference between the traditional experience of retirement, and the way many experience it today. It is the difference between a fairly orderly passage towards the long anticipated retirement and the very unsettling impact of the loss of job through redundancy. People in the former case have a long time to prepare their mind, and spirit, their family arrangements and money, their leisure plans and social activity. Responsibilities are gradually wound down. There is often a definite sense of fulfilment, that work has been satisfactorily completed, with a pension as a tangible expression of social approval. While it can still be a crisis point for many, highly disturbing as well as a great release, it is vastly different from redundancy.

After people have been declared redundant, I have seen emotional responses running from rage and anger, to depression and near paralysis. I have been in yards and plants while the names were typed, when personnel managers prepared themselves for harrowing interviews where tears would be shed by strong men.

Countless numbers of people have now been through that phase; through, also, the various phases which followed on into the period of actual severance from work, and on into the wilderness of the months and years afterwards. Much has been written about it, but still there is no normative process throughout industry to provide the necessary guidance and counselling which is so urgently required.

Influencing through Education and Training

There is always a careful balance to be struck between getting on with the actual job and that of reporting back, developing the understanding of others and providing education and training. For us, doing industrial mission has always been central, but the need to train others – theological students, priests and ministers in the Church – has also been recognised.

(a) *Theological Students*

The relationship between industrial mission and the theological colleges in Scotland has largely been dependent on the level of interest and understanding of the Professors of Practical Theology and their staff. In Glasgow and the West of Scotland, with its long industrial history and where industrial mission has been deeply rooted, one might have expected regular input into courses for divinity students. This however has never been the case. There were sporadic attempts, occasional lectures, a number of programmes planned, but that was all. In Edinburgh University's New College, on the other hand, there is still an annual industrial mission day conference, followed later in the week by a site visit. St Mary's College at St Andrews University and Christ College Aberdeen, have a lecture from industrial mission at least once in their theological courses. Programmes arranged for New College include Christian ministry and the significance of work for individuals and families, responsibilities of management and trade union officials, industrial mission and the Church's task in relation to unemployment, and industrial mission and the Church's task in relation to people at work.

On other occasions, managers, trade unionists and industrial missioners explored with students, after a brief theological and historical background to industrial mission, ministering to industrial people in the context of industrial change and some changes in the patterns of working life.

Sometimes the programme focused on current industrial events – for instance, on the significance of the privatisation of electricity production – and included speakers from the NUM and the electricity industry. Other programmes included perspectives of industrial mission from a quality assurance manager, a trade union official, and two part-time industrial chaplains. Others dealt with a theological perspective of employee and management relations, women and low pay, trade unions and management styles. Following the lectures students were taken to a number of different enterprises including Ethicon, the Scottish Gas Board, William Tyne, British Rail, Rowntree Mackintosh, Ferranti, and Scottish & Newcastle. It is difficult to estimate the value of those courses.

In many ways the students were already overloaded with a variety of subjects. The Industrial Day Conference and the visits were not regarded by them as a significant factor in their academic work. One obvious value lay in the mixture of students with experience of industry and commerce, and younger students without such experience. To those of us in industrial mission, one encouraging feature was the occasional meeting with students several years later when they expressed appreciation, now that they were parish ministers, of the insights they had gained. Indeed, a number later became part-time industrial chaplains.

(b) *At St Colm's College*

We also had some input into the training of students at St Colm's College where people are trained for non-ordained posts in the churches. The students would come to the industrial mission office in twos or threes each year and be encouraged to think of how the churches should deal with unemployment, or to reflect on changes in work practice and associated stress, and expressing Christian faith at work.

(c) *In-Service Courses for Ministers and Priests*

We have also tried to help ministers and priests working in urban parishes. Although not formally linked to a particular company, all of them work with people directly affected by the consequences of changes taking place in industrial society. In the mid and late 1980s we developed a series of in-service courses for clergy, some one day and others one week long. We shared a one week in-service training course for ministers at Stirling University with the Education Department of the Church of Scotland. It involved a number of visits to industrial sites in Central Scotland and was attended by some thirty ministers.

The Churches and Industrial Relations

There has always been close liaison between Industrial Mission and industrial relations specialists. They assist in the preparation of church statements on industrial issues. Every enterprise has its own industrial relations and the Advisory, Conciliation and Arbitration Service (ACAS) is always available if needed. It is very rare for full-time industrial chaplains to be drawn into the specifics of industrial relations, although it has happened. Sometimes the Church or its industrial chaplains have been expected to make a public statement. Occasionally, without knowledge of delicate discussions taking place between the disputing parties often under the auspices of ACAS, Church statements have appeared. While well intentioned, there are occasions when they were not appropriate either in content or timing, as a service to the disputing parties or to the wider community.

Industrial mission felt it wise to advise a simple procedure. An advisory pamphlet was prepared for those in the churches tempted to issue statements on industrial relations.

The Church's right to comment on moral or Christian grounds was always acknowledged, provided it understood the situation. This was not always as it appeared in the press or in the statements of one party or another. Sometimes those statements were deliberate bargaining gambits which both parties recognised as such, but which appeared to outsiders as dire threats with damaging consequences.

Occasionally, more than one church grouping was giving attention to the same dispute. Two very different statements could emerge on the same issue. Clearly, discussion would have been better conducted before, rather than after, the issuing of statements. In the interests of responsible and timely comment, industrial mission always felt it wiser for the churches, before commenting on industrial relations, first to contact the ecumenically-based industrial mission office. An introduction could usually be arranged, if necessary, between Church representatives and the appropriate parties, before intervention.

Industrial Mission National Conferences

The already mentioned Baird Hall Glasgow Conference of 1967 was a landmark for industrial mission in Scotland. There were a number of other major national conferences before the one held for Industry Year in 1986. In the early 1970s a conference was held in Glasgow on 'Man in the Making of the New Industrial Society', followed in May 1973 by 'Working Today for

Tomorrow', held at Napier College, Edinburgh. On 30 and 31 March 1979, 'Industry in the 80s' was held at Hamilton College of Education. These conferences tried to provide some guidelines for people who wanted to work for constructive change. Always there were preparatory groups working on aspects of the main themes. These included groups on: 'Christian Lifestyles in Industry Today', 'Power and Participation in Industry', 'Choices for Today to Build a Healthier Industrial Community', 'The Challenge of New Technology', and 'The Voice of the Unemployed'.

Again and again we were fortunate in having some of the most thought-provoking and visionary men and women to address our conferences. Some were Christians who wanted to apply biblical insights to the issues of industrial society. Others, though not professing Christians, were happy to work with us on these themes, which they also saw as significant.

I still have one leaflet for the Hamilton Conference, when our speakers were Dr Tom Johnston, Chairman of the MSC in Scotland; Andrew Neil, then Assistant Editor of *The Economist*; Lewis Robertson, Chief Executive of the Scottish Development Agency; Gavin Laird, then Scottish Executive Member of the AUEW; Allan Blacklaws, Group Personnel Director of Scottish & Newcastle; J B Smith, Assistant General Manager Ferranti Scotland; and one of our Manchester colleagues, Brian Cordingley, who was Team Leader there and also Secretary of the European Contact Group on Church and Industry.

That leaflet also had a short paragraph headed: 'Why is the Church running a Conference like this?' It said:

> Apart from anything else, if the Church is true to Jesus, it must be involved both in the day to day concerns of ordinary people and in the wider forces that shape and reshape their lives.
>
> Through the church's commitment of over one hundred industrial chaplains in Scottish Industry, during the past 35 years there has been built up a measure of trust and a network of contacts which provides a base from which to draw together a cross-section of our industrial community. It should be clear, however, that this conference is for all those who share our concern, whether church members or not. And the contributions of all will be equally valid.

Industrial Mission Gatherings

Such conferences were felt to be appropriate every few years or when either the industrial situation or the spirit of the times seemed to call for the substantial preparation they demanded. They were supplemented by industrial mission Gatherings. These were located in the areas in which full-time chaplains operated. They were intended to relate, though not exclusively, to the dominant industry of that area. Most of them took place while George Wilkie was National Organiser and his administrative assistance was available. We full-time chaplains provided lists of managers, trade unionists and others from church and industry, depending upon the theme. I can recall both useful and happy occasions in Greenock on shipbuilding, in Bathgate on the motor industry, in Hamilton on the steel industry, and in Kilmarnock on industrial relations. One in Glasgow, on transport, was held in Buchanan House, the headquarters of British Rail in Scotland. It focused on the special importance of transport for both the citizens and the life of a large city. People in responsible positions in British Rail, Glasgow Corporation Transport, Clyde Port Authority, and Freightliner, willingly co-operated.

In addition to seminar sessions, there was a two hour tour of strategic centres for transport and discussions about some of the basic human questions in relation to transport.

The Wallace Lectures

One of the pioneering industrial chaplains in Scotland was our much loved Cameron Wallace. In February 1962 he was inducted to the full-time chaplaincy to the shipyards and related industries on the Lower Reaches of the Clyde. He donned a boiler suit, a tammy and a clerical collar, and worked his way into the heart, mind and spirit of that dynamic area and the people who lived and worked within it. Partly for health reasons he moved to a small parish in Fife for the latter years of his ministry. When he died suddenly, quite early in his retirement, we decided to initiate, in grateful commemoration of his ministry with us, the Wallace Lectures.

The Links with The Advisory, Arbitration and Conciliation Service (ACAS)

ACAS continues to help industrial relations by counselling individuals and companies, and plays an important part in resolving industrial disputes. It produces a variety of publications which have been important for us in industrial mission. We have been fortunate in having excellent relations with successive Scottish Directors of ACAS and their staff. This has been valuable both informally, and in a number of industrial relations situations.

In 1986, during the *Daily Record* dispute, the ACAS Director, Matt Cochrane, was very angry at the intervention of the Iona Community and the Roman Catholic Church who had both appeared on television. Over lunch, Matt explained the delicate nature of negotiations and the fact that so often a stage was reached behind the scenes, which public interventions could make more difficult. During another major dispute, the company in dispute had refused to recognise ACAS. The trade unions asked me to liaise between union officers and the company directors. I was daily advised by ACAS. In order to ensure ecumenical co-operation, I had invited a Catholic and an Episcopal colleague to participate and I think we were able to help.

In recent years these informal relationships have continued to the point where we now have an annual meeting with the Director of ACAS, as well as informal contacts.

At Baxter House, an eventide home run by the Board of Social Responsibility of the Church of Scotland, the staff went on strike over the question of union recognition. Norman Orr's public statements and presence on the picket line led to a *contretemps* with Frank Gibson, the Director of Social Work for the Church of Scotland. The National Union of Public Employees asked the Church's General Assembly for recognition.

The Assembly remitted the matter to its Personnel Committee and I was asked to present a paper on trade unions and the Church to them. Later Alan Blacklaw, a lay member of the National Church and Industry Committee, Hugh Ormiston and I, met with them. We were able to resolve the matter amicably.

In 1987, I was asked by the National Union of Journalists (NUJ) to become involved with their dispute at the Scotsman Newspapers, and for a time, went between the union meeting in Picardy Place, in Edinburgh, and the Managing Director of Thomson Newspapers, the owners of *The Scotsman*. *The Scotsman* had refused to involve ACAS in the dispute, but I found it helpful to keep in touch with ACAS. As usual there is difficulty in knowing quite the value of our intervention. I had involved a local Episcopal rector, Canon Neville Chamberlain, and a Roman Catholic priest, Father Gerald Handy, both of whom shared the meetings with me. We helped them clarify a number of issues and eventually the dispute ended. Later, in 1990, industrial mission colleagues and I met with Mike Rowe, the new Director of ACAS in Scotland, who was interested in the Church's relationship with industry.

The International Christian Union of Business Executives (UNIAPAC)

In 1981, I went to Zurich to the biennial meeting of UNIAPAC. Through this organisation, chairmen and chief executives of European based multinational companies gathered to discuss the impact of their companies on society from a Christian perspective. Usually priests and ministers from most European countries were also invited. George Wilkie went in earlier years and I attended on three occasions, during one of which I led their Sunday worship. At another, the impact of multi-national companies on Third World countries was considered. The clash of cultures and social disturbance, in particular, were considered. I thought the Church was a bit like a multi-national company too!

CHAPTER 12

With Related Organisations

As Part of the Action of Churches Together (ACTS)

FOR years the key ecumenical body in the United Kingdom was the British Council of Churches (BCC). Unfortunately, while there were many areas of common concern and action between the Roman Catholic Church and the other churches, the former was not a member of the BCC. In Scotland the Catholic Church did share in the work of Scottish Churches House.

Following the lead of Cardinal Basil Hume at an ecumenical conference in Swanwick, the United Kingdom churches decided to create new ecumenical instruments, as they were called. This led to the inception of ACTS. Wisely, ACTS was to respond to ecumenical initiative at the local level. It would have a governing council and three major commissions. As National Organiser of industrial mission I was appointed by the Church of Scotland to the Commission on Social and Moral Issues where insights from working with industry could make a useful contribution.

Participating in the Centre for Theology and Public Issues (CTPI)

This centre was established within the University of Edinburgh, largely under the inspiration of Professor Duncan Forrester, the Professor of Christian Ethics and Practical Theology. It aims to stimulate reflection, discussion and research on important pubic issues to which theology may make a constructive contribution. The three successive organisers of industrial mission – George Wilkie, myself and Hugh Ormiston – have all served on the theological panel, and indeed all at the same time for a period. We found it valuable for our own thinking and believed that our experience with industry would be of value to the Centre.

The CTPI is chiefly interested in relations between structures, policies and practices on the one hand, and vision, values and assumptions on the other.

It tries to work at the meeting point of public, academic and Church life, bringing together groups of people to exchange knowledge. In that regard its methods are very similar to those of industrial mission, though dealing with a wider range of subjects. It works through conferences, consultations and seminars, through working groups operating often for two or three years on a particular theme, through occasional papers and books, and through a resource collection of printed material available to churches, researchers, and students. Occasionally it has employed a researcher for a specific task. In the years since its inception, the CTPI has played a constructive and helpful role in Scottish life, and its impressive list of publications continues to grow and be of value.

Sharing in Church Action on Poverty (CAP)

Industrial missioners, both in England and Scotland, were very much involved in the creation of CAP. It was formed in 1982 as a Christian-based ecumenical response to increasing levels of poverty in the UK. It informs people about the causes, the extent and the impact of poverty. It works for social change to assist the poor, to enable people in poverty to speak for themselves, to encourage dialogue between the powerless and the powerful, and to explore the links between faith and social action so as to maximise Church involvement in social justice issues. I can still see the flip charts which emerged in the discussions on these themes prior to the establishment of CAP!

Wealth creation brings both benefits and dis-benefits. The fruits of commerce and industry are bought at a high cost, and many people have been the victims of exploitation in the process.

In the UK, even today, some 14 million people live in households which have an income below half the average, which is a European measure for poverty. Since the mid 1970s, inequality has grown faster in the UK than in any other industrialised country except New Zealand.

Industrial mission must surely be concerned about the effects of poverty on individuals, families and communities. Poorer people have poorer health, reduced opportunities and lower life expectancy. While industrial mission's main focus remains the world of work, it cannot ignore poverty and unemployment. CAP also believes the restoration of hope and confidence and the rebuilding of community needs the direct involvement of the unemployed

The problem for industrial mission is of knowing how far to become involved in many of the social issues resulting from industrial change. We thought it appropriate to help create CAP, and have continued to support it. Several industrial missioners in England, and our own energetic Erik Cramb, have been particularly active. While approving this, it is not appropriate for industrial mission to focus on CAP or on poverty issues. Many others in the churches are better placed to do this.

Benefiting from the William Temple Foundation

Industrial mission in Britain has had a long association with the William Temple Foundation in Manchester, and owes a great deal to it. William Temple, an outstanding churchman and an Archbishop of Canterbury, died comparatively young in 1946. He was much concerned about the social issues of his day and, in many ways, ahead of his time. The Foundation established a college which was the first in Britain exclusively for women. It developed to include men, with a special emphasis on relating Christian faith to the secular world.

It was first located in Flintshire, but soon moved to Rugby where, in addition to its regular two year courses, it ran a wide variety of short courses and week-end conferences for industrial missioners and others. I count my three or four short stays there as helpful, both for the atmosphere of study linked to the outside world, and for my early encounters with industrial mission colleagues.

Courses also included managers, shop stewards and people from a wide variety of professional organisations. It was an institution of adult education, similar to lay academies in Germany and the Gossner Mission directed by Horst Symanowski.

The college moved to Manchester in 1971 where it became a 'college without walls', a phrase coined by David Jenkins, later to become Bishop of Durham. He was appointed Principal in 1973. How he managed the mixture of domestic life, academic life and the running of the Foundation, I do not know, but I recall him hard at work moving between our group and other tasks, while his daughter practised expertly on the piano in the rest room.

Roger Clarke, our chaplain in Dundee, had many useful gifts and it was no surprise when he accepted the invitation to become Associate Director of the William Temple Foundation along with David Jenkins. He helped develop the first induction courses for industrial chaplains. These still continue, and a number of the Scottish Team, including Erik Cramb, Duncan McClements and John Ross, have all attended.

While developing work in support of community involvement, and being of assistance to churches and clergy on a wide range of social and economic issues, the College maintains its strong links with industrial mission. One of its recent associate directors, Tony Addy, was seconded as secretary of the European Contact Group on industrial mission, a post which he still holds.

Influencing Society through The Society, Religion and Technology Project of the Church of Scotland (SRT)

Brief reference has already been made to the origins of SRT. It was at the 1968 Baird Hall Conference in Glasgow that Willie Robertson made his plea that the Church appoint someone to head up a project which would 'create an interface between technologists, theologians and other forward thinking people in Scotland'. The 1969 General Assembly agreed and early in 1970 the project was established. There was certainly a need for Christian ethical thinking on technological developments. Through working groups of experts, conferences and publications, it was hoped the project might act as a forum for discussion between the Church and specialist opinion in technology, and also stimulate public debate.

Its stated aim was: 'To foster an informed understanding in society of the issues which confront it as a result of current and future technologies and to inform the churches of key developments, to provide opportunities for technologists to reflect on the ethical implications of their work, to respond with considered judgement to Government bodies on technological issues, and to contribute actively to European and international debates on these issues.' There is no doubt the project has been highly successful in fulfilling those aims. Born out of industrial mission, but independent of it, industrial missioners have been rightly proud of its child.

Many in the wider church too recognise its value. The project has produced books, documents, reports, discussion papers and information sheets on a wide variety of topical issues. These have included the impact of the oil industry, nuclear and renewable energy, global warming, sustainable development, information technology and 'God and Science'. SRT is currently working on genetic engineering, transport, and environmental and technological education.

It has been blessed over the years by having the services of a wise advisory committee, firstly under the chairmanship of Dr Willie Robertson who was its guiding star from 1970 until June 1981. George Wilkie and Willie Robertson convened a group of very able people to guide the work of the project. Undoubtedly, the project was especially fortunate in having for its first director Dr John Francis, a nuclear scientist who was one of over a hundred very capable people who applied for the task. He was an Anglican, with not only a specific knowledge of his own field but a wide general knowledge of the impact of technological development on human life, plus considerable gifts of communication.

John acted as Director for two and a half years, during which he evolved a plan of overlap between outgoing and incoming directors. This has worked so well that the six directors who have led the project have carried on to completion the ongoing projects of their predecessors, while forging new lines of enquiry based on their own gifts and experience. George Wilkie was the industrial mission link with SRT until 1980 when I succeeded him, and so we have had ample opportunity to admire their work.

John Francis was Chairman of the Advisory Committee from 1981 to 1994 in succession to Willie Robertson, after which Professor John Eldridge of the University of Glasgow took over. The present Committee is enriched by the active involvement of Dr Alison Elliot, Dr Hugh Ormiston (continuing the industrial mission link), Charles Sommerville, now the sole remaining member of the original committee, Margaret Wallace, Dr John Francis, Dr Ruth Page of Edinburgh University, Professor David Atkinson, and the Revd Douglas Nicol, the Secretary of the Church of Scotland Board of National Mission.

Sharing in the Industrial Christian Fellowship (ICF)

Industrial mission in Scotland has benefited from a helpful association with the London-based Industry Christian Forum, formerly the Industrial Christian Fellowship, which has existed for over sixty years. It seeks to change attitudes towards the world of work by helping people find a fuller sense of God's purpose in their working lives. It helps Christians realise that in their work they serve both God and neighbour, and that faith, work and worship can be one. It encourages everyone to apply Christian values in their daily work, and helps people resolve the moral dilemmas they often face. The ICF exhorts the Church to support people in their work, and to declare the importance of all workers in generating wealth for the common good.

It tries to persuade industry, commerce and business to operate within a set of principles based on Christian teaching, arguing that these benefit employees, management, share-holders, suppliers, customers and the community. To achieve these aims, the ICF publishes training courses and training material for Church and business leaders. It produces worship material relating to the world of work, and offers practical support through its regional network. It publishes a widely regarded newsletter which often discusses important issues arising from the economy. At one time we co-operated with ICF in distributing in Scotland an ICF tabloid called *Monday*, but the contents were too London based to be of help and distribution ceased. Nevertheless we have had good working relations with a number of their secretaries and directors, including John Davis and David Arthur.

Supporting the European Contact Group (ECG)

In most European countries the churches have developed their own style of industrial mission. These developed in response to particular socio-economic, theological and ecclesiastical traditions. In Germany, lay academies are very important, including the Gossner Mission in Mainz. In France, there is the memory of the aborted worker priest project of the Catholic Church and the ongoing work of Mission Populaire de France, founded by a Scots Congregationalist, and working through worship centres and poor relief in down-town areas of French cities.

Some twenty years ago European industrial mission developed the ECG. It brings together individuals and organisations in the European churches active on questions of living and working conditions both in urban and rural areas. It has links with other ecumenical networks in Europe and to the World Council of Churches. It works with local people in urban, industrial and rural mission to develop international action through training, analysis and theological reflection. ECG sponsored initiatives work with unemployed people, with those on low pay, or with those who work in bad or insecure conditions. Emphasis is given to issues of housing and marginalisation, migrant workers and ethnic minorities.

International action is vital because economic and political structures increasingly operate across national boundaries through international agreements and strategies.

Cities face common problems of unemployment, pollution and poverty. Economics and politics throughout Europe are changing rapidly as the European Union continues to develop. Much legislation affecting living and working conditions originates with the European Commission and an effective response requires international co-ordination. Moreover, massive economic and political changes in middle Europe are creating new needs for international networking. The ECG has an important role in this new world.

CHAPTER 13

Participating
Churches

THERE are two large denominations in Scotland: the Church of Scotland and the Roman Catholic Church. The Church of Scotland has played a significant part in the development of industrial mission; and, in proportion to its size, so has the Methodist Church. The Catholic Church has traditionally seen the work as the responsibility of the laity.

The Methodist Church

Methodism in Britain has been for many years a strong supporter of industrial mission. There were a number of historical, theological and sociological reasons for this, but the driving force was the dynamic vision and character of Bill Gowland. After an effective ministry in Manchester, he went as Superintendent Minister to the Methodist Church in Luton. He had been stimulated by the Churches' Christian Commando Campaign at the end of the War, when a number of individual ministers had entered industry as chaplains in a largely unorganised and unco-ordinated way. At Luton he adapted his buildings so that, alongside the Methodist Church in Luton, a multi-storey college aimed at undergirding and supporting the Church's work in relation to industry was built. From this centre Methodist industrial mission has been co-ordinated and supported ever since.

Because of the size of the Methodist Church in the UK, Bill Gowland saw that the number of full-time industrial chaplains would never be more than eight or nine, with scope for many more part-time chaplains. The programmes arranged at Luton were designed to assist both chaplains and Christians at work. Events and discussions were held at weekend conferences on a wide range of subjects. A range of councillors drawn from industry and the academic world gave time to lecture at the College until its closure in 1996.

In Scotland there had always been a few Methodist chaplains, but no likelihood of a paid appointment. When I was first appointed to the work, there was a Methodist minister in Partick, the Superintendent of the Glasgow West circuit, from whom I gained much support. Through working with him, Bill Gowland came to visit us in our home in Glasgow.

I asked him to send someone to Glasgow who had some experience of industrial mission. Fortunately he was able to arrange for the half-time chaplain in Coventry to be appointed to Maryhill Methodist Circuit. This was John Potter, who quickly began to share in industrial mission in Glasgow as chaplain to Queen Street Station. Sometime later, when Sandy Ryrie took ill and had to leave the post of industrial chaplain in North Lanarkshire, John was appointed by the Church of Scotland to succeed him.

Meanwhile, partly to balance the Church of Scotland's employment of John Potter, Bill Gowland agreed to appoint Jim Mack, a Methodist minister, first as half-time chaplain in Glasgow and later full-time. On his retiral, Jim Mack was succeeded by Harold Clarke.

After 17 years in Scotland, Harold followed Bill Gowland as Principal of Luton Industrial College; and first Allan Wright, then Bill Rayne, became the Methodist full-timer in Scotland.

The Congregational Union

This is a church of a similar size to that of the Methodist church in Scotland. The Methodist commitment of a full-time chaplain in Scotland was funded from a UK Methodist Home Mission source. The Congregational Union of Scotland, however, is a Scottish based set of churches made up essentially of separate independent congregations. It made a distinctive contribution to industrial mission in Scotland. Stimulated in part by an excellent survey of the economic situation made one year to its assembly, a few of its ministers became part-time chaplains.

One of these, David Laing, then minister of the Congregational Church in Govan, joined the small nucleus of the Glasgow industrial mission team which I was trying to develop. We met weekly to think, work and plan an appropriate industrial mission programme. David took a leading part.

Later, when David was called to the sprawling Easterhouse estate, the Congregational Union joined in a new experiment. Its General Secretary and I shared in inducting David to the joint task of industrial mission in Glasgow and Congregational ministry in Easterhouse. Through his commitment to politics he was elected to Strathclyde Region where he became well-known for his distinguished leadership as Convener of the vast Social Work Committee.

Other Congregational ministers have played their part well as part-time chaplains. Stanley Britton of the Congregational Church in Hawick has been, for 15 years, a member of the National Church and Industry Committee. He acted as Area Organiser for the Borders until his retirement. Today he continues as a local chaplain in Barrie Knitwear, Hawick.

The Scottish Episcopal Church

In England the major component of industrial mission has always been provided by the Church of England. The regional structure of industrial mission in England is largely shaped by diocesan boundaries. In Scotland the relatively small Scottish Episcopal Church has played a part in the work. Before I became a full-time chaplain in Glasgow, there had been a short period when an Episcopal priest, I think by the name of John Hullsay of Roslyn Chapel, was chaplain to the coal industry in the area. George Wilkie referred to him as one of the full-time staff. On the National Church and Industry Committee, the Episcopal Church was represented by a retired layman.

After the post of Industrial Youth Chaplain was advertised, we appointed a young Episcopal priest, Jim Kay – although it was not an appointment made by the Episcopal Church. In 1985 it did appoint a half-time chaplain, John Walker, who was priest in charge of a small parish in Dundee, and half-time industrial chaplain alongside John Ross for a number of years.

For a period the Episcopal Church's Board of Social Responsibility reserved £3000 for industrial mission work, preferably for use with the unemployed, but this never developed into a practical commitment. Nevertheless the Episcopal Church is still represented on the National Church Industry Committee and on local area committees. It assists with the administration of the part-time chaplaincy at South Gyle in Edinburgh, and I am sure if it had been larger and more evenly spread through the industrial areas of Scotland it would have played a fuller part

The Roman Catholic Church

There has not been a time during the past twenty years when there was not at least some sharing by the Roman Catholic Church in Scotland in industrial mission. I have mentioned that in the earlier days of my own appointment I was encouraged by Father Vincent Cowley. He was a core member of a Roman Catholic organisation called the Industrial Research Information Service (IRIS). Its aim, which I thought misguided, was to ensure the success at trade union elections, of candidates who would win against communist candidates.

Many trade unions in those days – including the NUM, the T&GWU and the AEU, were racked by right and left wing battles for supremacy. IRIS was seen to support the right wing. We argued a lot about this, but in spite of that, as Christians, we had many other views in common. He, his assistant, Jack Brennan and myself, sometimes with other Catholic laymen, worked well together on a number of projects.

A young Catholic priest, Frank Kennedy, working in Yoker, attended one of our early industrial mission courses at Glasgow University. From that day, for over ten years, he became an invaluable member of the Glasgow team. His intellect, humour and gracious personality would have made him an asset anywhere. Already equipped with high academic qualifications in philosophy, he was soon appointed a lecturer in philosophy at St Peter's Theological College. He continued with industrial mission, however, and through him the Roman Catholic Diocese of Glasgow learned of industrial mission. He once addressed a large gathering in the MacLellan Galleries in Glasgow on the significance of the Papal Encyclical '*Laborem Exercens*'. He struggled weekly with us in developing the most appropriate response to a range of industrial events and sometimes involved shipyard workers in the process. When he left industrial mission and the Glasgow Diocese to serve in the Argentine, he wrote a most thoughtful book on industrial mission called *God's Working World*. We hoped the diocese would find someone to follow him, but they were unsuccessful.

The predominant view of the Roman Catholic Church, and of many priests, is that the parish is the main agency of the Church's work. Later, when I was seeking funding for the post in Glasgow of industrial youth chaplain, I was delighted to find that Archbishop (as he was then) Tom Winning was able to provide, from diocesan funds, 25 % of the funds for the post.

In Aberdeen, when we were beginning the oil chaplaincy, Bishop Mario Conti and a number of Roman Catholic laymen encouraged us. There have always been a few priests working as voluntary chaplains, and a number of lay people on the National Church and Industry Committee. Moreover, within industry, there have been Catholic people, almost instinctively, valuing and supporting the work of industrial mission and regretting the apparent absence of support from their Church.

CHAPTER 14

Work-life expands
to fill many Corners

I SUPPOSE for any busy life to be at all useful, work must be arranged in
some order of priority. For me now, writing this inadequate record, the
question is what to omit. There were many events, occasions and programmes
which took time, effort and planning, which cannot find a place here but I now
recall and note a few which might simply be listed as a miscellany.

Visiting Ireland

In September 1981, I was invited to Belfast and Londonderry by the Irish
Churches' Central Council for Community Work. We held a conference at each
of these cities on 'Unemployment', the 'Evaluation of Life at a Time of No
Work', and 'Some Practical Responses of the Church to Unemployment'.
Due to the Troubles, the Irish churches had given little time to industrial
mission and unemployment. They were very interested to hear of our methods.

The Churches' Central Council for Community Work was one of the
very few organisations in Northern Ireland that did operate with the co-operation of all of the churches. Bishop Daly was present, as were the leaders of
other churches, trade union officials, community workers, a number of police
and a variety of people from the churches. In earlier years, many of my own
friends were Irish and spoke with the same accent as I was hearing during that
short visit. There was a sense of kinship with everyone I met, but it was sad
to discover that they all had personal experience of the war in Ireland and most
of them had been close to death. I remember at one point moving a few
chairs and discovering, to the chagrin of the owner, a revolver had dropped
out of his jacket pocket hanging on the back of a chair!

The statutory and voluntary structures for dealing with unemployment
were unlike those in Scotland. So also was the delivery of training and industrial development. There was value in the cross fertilisation of ideas, and it
was certainly salutary to me to see their courage and faith. Running with a

small group of people for shelter during a heavy downpour in Londonderry, I found myself huddling beside two English soldiers in their military capes, but with rifles at the ready.

Briefing Church of Scotland Moderators

One of the tasks of the industrial mission Organiser is to brief the Moderator when he is likely to be visiting an industrial site or when he has been urged to make a public statement. There was a period in the early and mid 1980s when massive industrial change, large scale closures of major industries and huge redundancies, made it important for the Church to show concern for the people involved and the new society being created.

Journalists always found it difficult to deal with a church like the Church of Scotland. They much prefer bishops so that they can readily report from a recognised 'church leader'. Our custom of appointing a Moderator for a year, who is the Moderator only of the General Assembly of the Church, was sometimes difficult for them to understand, not least because he is not seen by Church of Scotland people as a church leader in the sense of a bishop. He is certainly a representative Church figure.

At the beginning of his one year period of office, industrial mission and members of the Church and Nation Committee often provided material on which the Moderator drew for a statement. This might be unsatisfactory, not least because journalists tended to follow the Moderator after his term of office was over when he could give only his own opinion. On one or two occasions, his opinion did not coincide with that of the General Assembly. Accordingly, we encouraged the Press to look not so much to the Moderator, but to the Convener of the Church and Nation Committee for statements from the Church of Scotland.

At times, statements made jointly by the Moderator, the Chairman of the Catholic Bishops' Conference, and the Primus of the Scottish Episcopal Church, were used.

In 1985, I briefed a Moderator on his visit to the CBI in London. A year later we began the practice of holding a briefing session for the incoming Moderator. This gave him an overall picture of our contacts with industry. We were able to give him an indication of some of the issues that might be arising in the coming year. That same year I briefed the Moderator for a visit to the STUC and went with him. In October, I accompanied him on a visit to Strathclyde Fire Service with Peter Houston, the Fire Brigade chaplain. Earlier in the year we had arranged a useful meeting between the Moderator and the Director of the NCB in Scotland.

Eventually, through the courtesy of each successive Moderator, we arranged that a representative group of people from industry should gather annually at the Moderator's flat in Charlotte Square Edinburgh, for an informal reception. These meetings with groups of people from many different commercial sectors were valuable in themselves and also helped in the general growth of the work of industrial mission.

The Lockerbie Disaster

Shortly before the tragic explosion in Scottish skies of the PanAm aeroplane which so suddenly shattered the peace of Lockerbie and the world, the full-time team had been reflecting on lessons to be learned by the churches from the earlier Chinook helicopter crash and the Piper Alpha tragedy. Andrew Wylie had been closely involved with both. A few days after Piper Alpha, I had gone with him to spend some time with the crew of the twin platform. We recognised how inadequate the response to these events was. Andrew later wrote thoughtful and valuable papers on the subject.

Already it was apparent that when major disasters strike, public awareness and media hype brought about an unhealthy rush of so-called 'experts' in disaster counselling onto the scene. The Church and its ministers are all too familiar with the call to respond to illness, accident, death and bereavement. But we had to accept that we were less than prepared for major events like these. Wise and sensitive procedures had to be established and the churches had to be part of them.

The test came too soon. Early on the morning of the Lockerbie crash, I suggested to the Church of Scotland's Principal Clerk, Jim Weatherhead, and to Jim Whyte, the Moderator, that we should ensure good Church support. It would be wise to make sure that Sandy McDonald, Secretary of the Ministry Department, and Ian Doyle, Secretary of the Board of National Mission, arranged assistance for local ministers and churches who had been thrown into new pastoral tasks made more difficult because the eyes of the world were on them.

They coped well, as did so many at that trying time. The world heard the best of straightforward but profound Scottish preaching, through the words and grace of Jim Whyte, and we were all grateful to him. I recall being visited by someone who had a police connection with the Lockerbie event, who said that while the army chaplains were supporting young soldiers dealing with the shattered remains of human bodies, the police had no such support. Many questions remain, even today, as to whether we are ready and how we in the churches ought to respond to what seems like an increasing number of similar disasters.

Since Lockerbie, a 'disaster industry' with its own 'experts' travelling around offering help seems to have developed. Perhaps they are needed. But it must also be recognised that the single unreported injury or death, the small unreported industrial accident, still has its own need for skilled and sensitive pastoral care.

The East African Steam Engine Project

It may seem odd today to have a section in this book about a steam engine, and yet this project received sustained attention from industrial mission.

The story goes as far back as the turn of this century, when a company in England, Peter Brotherhood, designed what they called a 'type 42 steam engine'. In Edinburgh, Maxwell Davidson of Maxwell Davidson Consulting Engineers believed that this engine could be adapted for use in Third World countries. Springburn in Glasgow had been, at one time, a world centre for the manufacture and repair of steam engines. The closure of the last works was a major blow to the area. Shortly after that closure, Norman Orr joined the new Springburn Churches' Enterprise Group set up to create jobs on the vacant site. They set about seeking suitable projects.

Norman, who was himself an engineer, worked with Maxwell Davidson to modify and develop a boiler to raise steam for the type 42 engine to enable it to drive a generator for use in Third World countries.

The Springburn Churches' Enterprise Group transferred their interest in the project to industrial mission as the only other group in the church likely to have the interest and ability to complete the project. The Industrial Mission Trust guaranteed a loan from the Ecumenical Development Co-operative Society to allow local people to work on the project. Eventually the equipment was demonstrated at Eldoret in Kenya. It could produce power for refrigeration, irrigation, electric lighting, and many other purposes.

A company was formed with four partners – the Board of National Mission of the Church of Scotland, industrial mission, Maxwell Davidson Consulting Engineers Ltd, and Glasgow North and Strathclyde Community Enterprise – and a year later it was taken over entirely by Maxwell Davidson Consulting Engineers. They are still refining the system and it is hoped that the vision and the effort put into it will one day be of benefit to many people.

Visitors to Industrial Mission in Scotland

It is difficult to recall our many visitors. They came to see how we operated, to ask for training and experience, and even for placements within industry alongside our work. We always found value in meeting people, lay and ordained, who like us were concerned to take the insights of the Gospel into the world of industry and commerce.

For several years, six of our Norwegian colleagues working in the Norwegian sector of the North Sea came to Aberdeen, where Andrew Wylie and Donald Rennie had arranged a varied programme for them. The main value lay in the interaction between Christian ministers of different churches. Our Norwegian colleagues were Lutheran ministers employed by the Norwegian Seamen's Mission.

The pastor of the German congregation in Glasgow, Herbert Gunneberg, who later became a minister of the Church of Scotland, was one of many German ministers influenced by Horst Symanowski, the leader of the Gossner Mission to industry in Germany. On three occasions he asked me to receive German colleagues and to show them something of our work. On the third occasion we took them and their wives to various parts of Scotland where my colleagues had arranged a full programme of events for them.

A New Zealand Salvation Army Captain, who had been appointed to industrial mission in Dunedin, visited our work in 1983. I can recall his surprise at confronting for the first time a Scottish kipper, and Hugh recalls our visitor's unfortunate claustrophobia which prevented him visiting the coal-face at Solsgirth mine in Fife.

Harry Daniels was the World Council of Church's Secretary for Urban and Industrial Mission in Geneva. He was Burmese and later became a bishop of the Church of South India in Madras. He stayed with us during his visit to Scotland, a visit made memorable by his gracious presence with us in the team.

It was even more memorable for a small domestic matter. Wanting a shower in the morning, he called down in his white robe to ask how to turn on the hot water. To our embarrassment there had been an electrical fault during the night and no power meant no hot water.

Felix Sugirtaraj, a young industrial missioner from the South Indian state of Coimbatore, visited us; as did a Spanish worker priest, and Pere Tacceon, a worker priest from France. Pere Tacceon wanted to meet shop stewards in Glasgow and I took him to a number of plants, including Davy United, and Mavor and Coulston.

One evening I arranged a meeting in the house for a mixed group of managers and stewards. Pere Tacceon spoke little English and the stewards and managers spoke little French. I invited Dr Munn, Headmaster of Cathkin High School in Rutherglen, who was fluent in French and a member of the church we attended. His struggle was not with the translation, but with expressing fairly radical ideas passing between the Scottish shop stewards and the worker priest.

For a time there were annual visits of members of the French Protestant Industrial Mission.

Many of our English and Welsh colleagues have also been with us. We gained much from their visits, while they, we hope, gained something from visiting Scotland. My wife and I still recall with amusement the evening I brought home two young East African industrial missioners. They had just stepped into the hall when one of them suddenly said, 'What's that?' Our two boys were watching a television programme called 'Daktari', a series about care of animals in East Africa. Someone on the series had said loudly in Swahili, 'Welcome to this home'. No wonder the young Kenyan was surprised!

A recurring feature was the arrival in Edinburgh of industrial missioners on sabbatical tours from other parts of the world. Many of them wanted to study industrial mission in Europe and to see how we went about things in Scotland. There was Ouasi from Ghana, whom each of us took for a Monday during his time at New College; David Markstone of Queensland, with us for two weeks as part of a Churchill study tour; and Sister Julia McLaughlin of Kent Industrial Mission. There was also a visit from the Indonesian Council of Churches. They remained in our Glasgow office for a day discussing relations between Church, politics and industry. A delegation of Chinese government officials came. They visited Scotland at the same time as events were taking place in Tiananmen Square.

Work and Faith

I was grateful to Peter MacDonald, Editor of *Life and Work*, for publishing a series of articles on the Gospel and daily life. We know most Christians find it extremely difficult to make an effective link between faith and work. I could quote dozens of situations like the two that I give.

At a kirk session of sixty elders, one man said during discussion, 'I have to take off my Church hat on a Sunday night because I have to be a different kind of animal on Monday morning'. Two men who worked in the same office for ten years were amazed to learn they were both active members of their respective churches.

We ought to be able to bridge the gap between two vitally important dimensions of life which are intertwined – work and faith. Our training, our hours of work, pay, technical competence, and job security, are all vital to us. For many our lives are shaped by our work. How strange that there should be such an enormous gap between our work and our Christian faith!

Life and Work's Editor asked me to deal specifically with the situation of people working on the shop floor, but the 'shop floor' nowadays rises to many levels. A director can find him or herself carefully negotiating with the shop floor against 'faceless and callous bosses' further up the corporate tree.

Some people imagine trade union activity is incompatible with the Gospel. When we published George Wilkie's book, *The Role of Christians in Trade Unions,* Len Murray, then General Secretary of the TUC, wrote in the foreword: 'This little book states that a person's Christian faith will affect his judgement of issues and his support of policies. Precisely! .... and that is why he (and she) must bring faith and Christian insights to bear on the great decisions and the great choices which, for better or for worse, trade unions help to make in our society and our world.'

Later he told me he had been very encouraged, as a Christian, that the Church of Scotland had published this booklet.

I recall another kirk session where a moderate trade union leader was an elder. He told me with wry humour and sadness that the other elders insisted on calling him 'the Wee Red'. Another shop steward frequently said to me, 'Look, we are taught in the Church about stewardship. Well I see my job as a shop steward as a Christian responsibility!'

Justice often requires conflicts, industrial disputes, and even strikes, and Christians who are affected must not run away from them. An emphasis on the Christian growth and development of the individual, within churches, has often ill-equipped us for a world where people live and work in groups.

Most organisations have have two inter-connecting structures – one informal and the other formal. Most people have informal links with about a dozen others. Beyond that group is a larger network of relationships often between people of different responsibilities and remuneration. Morale, work atmosphere and inter-personal relationships are all coloured by the interaction of the groups.

Surely that is a sphere where the Christian can make a positive contribution, not by buttonholeing techniques or church talk, but by shedding the light of Christ on issues that arise in conversation.

There is also the formal structure of a work organisation. Organisational ethos is vital and often depended, historically, on management/union relations. These are changing quite dramatically while unions themselves are declining in size. One study of people at work produced the following statement: 'As Christians we accept responsibility in management in the light of Christ; as Christians we accept responsibility as workers' representatives in the light of Christ.' Christians in these difficult and changing times face the same dilemmas as others.

Recently I spoke with a number of Christians in a very large company where the employees were being balloted on industrial action. They had to balance the need of the company, on which their own future depended, with the need to push for improved wages and conditions. Christians must not contract out of the responsibility of participating in this sphere. Jesus spent a great deal of his ministry dealing with the real situations in which people actually lived and insisted that these situations were His and the Father's concern. We must avoid the mistake of imagining God is only concerned with the Church. While He may work through the Church for the sake of the world, He is already in the world.

A German industrialist asked a young chaplain what he was seeking to do. 'I am taking God into industry!' answered the chaplain happily. 'And where are you taking Him next?' asked the industrialist. God has a continuing task for those who wish to live an authentic Christian life in the workplace. It is a Gospel responsibility to work for a healthy, safe, just, humane and Christ-like working world.

CHAPTER 15

Industrial Mission
and Trade Unions

Working with the Scottish Trade Union Congress (STUC)

IN addition to links with many individual trade unions and shop stewards, works conveners and trade councils, industrial mission has always had a good relationship with the STUC. In many ways the STUC intertwines with the public life of Scottish society to a greater extent than the British TUC. It has been fortunate in its last two General Secretaries, James Milne and Campbell Christie. The STUC has to be ready to respond to a wide range of industrial incidents and crises at a moment's notice. Invariably they have been successful in clarifying issues and underlining the importance of workers' rights, employment needs, and training needs.

On many occasions the STUC has invited industrial mission to participate in its conferences, although often at short notice. Our committee structure sometimes made it difficult for us to respond quickly and, as a result, the churches' contribution was sometimes inadequate.

At one point, in 1984, Hamish Morrison, James Mack, James Milne and myself met on several occasions to discover how industrial mission and the churches, the STUC, and the SCDI, could effectively contribute to the debate about trends in Scottish industrial life. While this might not always have developed into any agreed plan, a mutual confidence developed. After Campbell Christie was appointed, he met with industrial mission and we have continued to meet annually with the General Council to discuss areas of mutual interest.

Industrial Mission and the Trades Councils

The STUC has been an important organisation serving the needs of working people for all of a hundred years. It developed from trades councils which have an even longer history. They continue to this day, while to some extent searching for new purpose and identity. As at the national level trade unions join to form the TUC, at the local level they combine to form trades councils. They provide a forum for representatives of trade union branches to formulate policy on industrial, social and community issues. In Scotland they are affiliated directly to the STUC and send delegates to the annual Congress, but in England they are not directly involved in the TUC. They cannot instruct union branches, but act as a co-ordinating body.

They also provide help and advice to union branches, act as the local voice of the STUC, work to improve economic and social conditions, and comment on matters of industrial, social and community interest.

Industrial mission has always had contacts with the many trades councils. When I first attended the monthly meetings of the Glasgow Trades Council, I was struck with the similarities between it and Glasgow Presbytery. Apart from the pall of smoke in their meeting place, there were the same argumentative West of Scotland voices. Where in one the focus was on jobs, trade reports and pay, the other considered church membership, mission activity, the life of congregations and the wider Church. Both ranged meticulously through reports on current problems and, therefore, over very much the same issues.

Such is the tragic separation between Church people and active trade unionists, it is likely few presbytery members ever set foot in a trades council meeting, and few active trade unionists experienced the cut and thrust of a presbytery.

In July 1995 a survey of trade council activity revealed that the work of the 34 trade councils in Scotland varied considerably. Now there is a move to change the name to trade union councils, and thought of a special year to promote their developments. Whatever the future, their past has been a very useful one.

Trade Unions Decline

By the early 1990s, traditional industries – including steel making, coal, shipbuilding and textiles – had all but disappeared from Scotland. Defence related industries watched their markets decline.

Inward investing companies brought new jobs, as well as new approaches to employee relations. In all sectors a new awareness of labour costs led to fewer employees and improvements in productivity. Trade union membership fell to 8.2 million. Only a third to two-fifths of the British labour force were members of trade unions, which was a decrease of 10 % compared with ten years ago. Increasingly, companies were resisting union recognition, some even de-recognising unions they had dealt with over a very long time. Nissan, Toyota and Panasonic signed single union agreements. Trade unions were forced to examine their own purposes and structures. Some made a number of their own staff redundant and nearly all began to explore providing financial and other services to their members.

Increasing emphasis is being put on recruitment with particular concern for women and ethnic minorities, and unions continue to amalgamate. Three unions joined to form the new Broadcasting Entertainments Cinematograph and Theatre Union. The Society of Graphical Artists and the National Graphical Association united to form the new Graphical Paper and Media Union for the printing industry. There were also mergers in clothing, textiles and footwear to form the new National Union of the Footwear, Leather and Allied Trades and several hosiery and knitwear unions joined the General Municipal and Boilermakers Union; and there were many others.

The Bargaining Atmosphere Changes

The recession of the late 1980s and early '90s undoubtedly tempered employee demands. In some companies pay increases were frozen and performance-related pay schemes grew in popularity. The length of the working week again became an important issue and the AEEU organised a highly successful campaign which achieved a significant reduction in it. Annualised hours to reduce overtime costs were increasingly adopted.

Employees were frightened to take collective action, while companies began to attack collective bargaining.

The 1980s was a difficult decade for trade unions throughout the industrialised world. The average share of trade union membership among all employees across ten OECD member countries fell from 35 % in 1980, to 28% in 1988. A key factor in the decline of membership of trade unions in OECD countries, and particularly in the UK, was the result of the very sharp rise in unemployment. The losses in the 1980s took place in the more highly unionised countries of the UK, Australia and Italy, but unions have registered gains in membership and collective-bargaining successes in less developed countries to which companies have fled in search of cheap labour. There has been, for instance, a rapid growth of trade unionism in Brazil, South Africa and South Korea.

Trade Unionism and the TUC

In July 1992, Gillian Sheppard, the Employment Secretary, signalled the Government's intention to end its 13 year stand-off with the trade unions. She intended to complete the passage into legislation of the measures contained in the White Paper, 'People, Jobs and Opportunity', which she inherited from Michael Howard. She had no plans to add to its provisions, but said the decline of industrial unrest was evidence of a sea change in industrial relations in Britain. That year fewer working days were lost to strikes than at any time since the 1920s. The legislation contained provisions which were criticised by trade unions, for it would end the check-off arrangements under which companies collected union dues. It would also give employees the right to belong to any union, and trade unionists feared it would lead to a steep fall in membership. The Bill also required unions to give advance notice of strikes. In the event, only some of these fears were realised.

The position of the TUC underwent considerable internal discussion and questioning. Only a few years ago it had been a powerful central voice for trade unionism and an essential ingredient in the corridors of power in White-hall. It was criticised for issuing rather bureaucratic documents. Some wanted it to target key areas – such as health and safety and the deepening social divide – and it appeared slow to respond to events. There was a painful staff reduction of 20 % to save money and the role of the TUC itself was questioned.

In 1992 the National Executive Committee of the Labour Party unanimously decided to cut the unions' voting share from 90 % to 70 %. This led to a decline of union influence in Party leadership elections, in selecting parliamentary candidates, and in changing policy. These were all areas in which the unions had had a strong voice. Meanwhile, the STUC and the Scottish Federation of Small Businesses agreed to draw up a code of practice designed to promote good industrial relations within the small business world.

CHAPTER 16

Both Industrial
and Mission

Industrial Mission within the Wider Work of the Church

IN a newsletter for Christians in industry, an article appeared under the heading 'What is Industrial Mission?' It began by saying that for those not familiar with industrial mission, there may appear to be missing ingredients. Industrial mission had not spelt out, but assumed, that as individual Christians we should seek to grow in grace and engage in personal witness for Christ within our work as well as at home.

By contrast, the statement which had been worked out carefully by the Churches Consortium on Industrial Mission, adopted in 1977 and accepted by the Scottish National Church and Industry Committee, read:

Industrial mission is part of the total mission of the Church. It is concerned to further the purpose and work of God as made known in Christ, within industry and industrial society.

Industrial mission is a Christian activity which lay and ordained men and women share together. It involves taking part in the conversations which occur in the industrial world, being sensitive to what is happening and seeking to understand.

Through the process of participation, reflection and evaluation, industrial mission works for the embodiment of Christian values in the relationships, methods and goals of industry and commerce; industrial mission seeks also to interpret this work, and what is discovered, in its consequences for the Church at large.

In essence, it is a part of the normal work of the churches, but it is firmly outward looking and related to society at large. Since it is part of the mission of Christ, it needs the guidance, direction and presence of the Holy Spirit.

The aims of industrial mission are to ensure the formation of a competent, sensitive and credible Christian presence within the world of work. This includes supporting people at work by searching for insights and shared experience within industry and the Church. It insists that Christian discipleship includes mature and responsible Christian thought and action within the corporate and collective structures of industrial society. It tries to pay careful attention to the character of events and to their movement with regard to employment, to discern the signs of the Kingdom, and to call all to an appropriate response. It also promotes human fulfilment in partnership with God to express the work of his creation.

Those committed to Christ and involved in the mission and ministry of the Church are often highly motivated. We are certainly not unaware of the immensity and difficulties of our task. We long for others to respond to Christ's call. Essential to the proclamation of the Gospel is the invitation to personal commitment to Christ. Yet the immediacy of the demands upon us often prevents us from standing back a little and reflecting on the nature of the task and its changing priorities. There must, therefore, be a prayerful, worshipping and responsive Christian community where, through the means of grace, new Christians are sustained and nourished to become mature enough to go out themselves and share in witness and mission. Witness to what? Mission in what?

Few of us would be satisfied with a spiral of mission which began and ended in conversion-nurture-church-evangelism-conversion-nurture-church … evangelism … and so on. We believe the Gospel points to a light, a salt, a leaven, within the world for which Christ died.

The Christian mission field in any human society does not remain the same for very long. While there are some unchanging features, hardly a parish is the same as it was ten or twenty years ago.

Industrial Mission as Part of Mission

It may be helpful to trace here a little of the roots of industrial mission for those less familiar with it. It began with the recognition that massive numbers of our people were untouched, in key areas of their lives, by the Christian Gospel. Their work shapes and makes possible family and domestic life. The German pastor who set up industrial mission in Germany did so from the stark recognition that his church, adjacent to a large factory, was not even being noticed by the 7000 workers who daily passed its doors. 'Was the Gospel noticed?' he wondered. 'How are industrial life and its issues to be influenced by the light of Christ?'

Simon Phipps, in *God on Monday*, wrote of the way the Gospel for God's world had implications for the Church's task: 'At times the Church has pre-supposed that it knows what the Gospel is for in secular situations, from an ecclesiastical base outside. We are all familiar with a type of limpet-bomb evangelism, whereby the Gospel is stuck onto the outside of a situation, in the hope that it will go off with a bang and stir things up inside, while the evangelists run for cover.' Phipps believes 'it is no good shouting the Gospel over the fence, out of the Church into the world. Such a Gospel remains in inverted commas. For the true Gospel is the Word of God, and God is inside the fence already, speaking his Word there in the world'.

In Scotland, experience of ministers in wartime, chaplaincies in factories, and hydro camps, and in Christian commando campaign visits to steel works, led to a recognition of the need to take industry, and the people within it, more seriously than had been the case.

There has always been an obvious need for mission in schools, universities, prisons, hospitals, and other institutions dealing with the young and the needy – ministering to people in their need. Industrial mission, on the other hand, is about ministering to people in their strength, even though industrial life is full of tensions that are the cause of deep wounds at the personal level. Industrial mission's most widely accepted definition, which begins with the same words as the CCIM statement of 1977, states:

Industrial mission is part of the total mission of the Church. It is concerned to further the purpose and work of God, as made known in Christ, within industrial society, and to help the Church at large to see involvement in industrial and economic affairs as an essential part of its mission.

Industrial mission is a Christian activity which lay and ordained men and women share together. It involves taking part in the conversations which occur in the industrial world, being sensitive to what is happening and seeking to understand.

Industrial mission aims to discover the effect of industry on the people who work in it, the society which depends on it, and the world order which is being shaped by it. Industrial mission works for the re-ordering of the relationships, methods and goals of industry and commerce, in the light of the Christian hope for justice and community, and through the process of participation, reflection and evaluation.

Another helpful statement came some years ago from the World Council of Churches' Advisory Group on Urban and Industrial Mission:

Industrial mission really means the presence of the Christian community at points of need and tension, as well as of creativity and decision, so that Christians engage in issues, events and structures for the sake of the Gospel.

The core of Christian mission is Christian community, not isolated individuals or institutional ministries. New Christian communities need to be created to coincide with secular structures. Christian mission is best accomplished by people indigenous to a situation, a locality, or a structure. The churches must recruit and commit Christians within all areas of modern life. At the same time, Christians must recognise and be thankful that many of God's agents of humanisation are not a part of the Church.

Christian participation in humanising programmes usually means co-operating with others more competent and equally dedicated, together in the action of God. Priorities for local strategy mean the most effective agents of mission are persons, groups and structures familiar with the scene.

The task is to find and prepare such indigenous agents. It is not enough to provide some specialised services. Mission is the expression of the total being of the Church. It therefore involves, above all, the laity of the Church. Ecumenical co-operation and planning leading to joint action for mission are not optional extras but a basic necessity.

It is difficult to take Gospel to the complicated issues of our working life. Some Christians find it too difficult and turn inwards, using it only for private and family life. Others draw on their Christian resources for analysis of major issues, such as environment, racialism, peace and the arms race. Work life is too often neglected.

We have had a long period of Church history in which the relation between faith and work was neglected. This is surprising in view of the pervasive Christian belief, before and since the Reformation, that the Gospel is for the whole of life. People have the opportunity of participating in the shaping of God's world. In human relationships, in the informal and formal structures of industry, in the decision-making, styles of leadership, and team co-operation, our faith is an ingredient of the whole. It is the task of industrial mission to help Christians understand this better.

Industrial Mission challenged

Those of us working in industrial mission over many years have found it difficult to fault this concept of mission. It is biblically and theologically sound, although its practice has always been difficult to develop. Of course, there are Christians working within all the structures and institutions of our society. Some understand they are called to seek to influence the goals, methods and relationships of their organisations in a Christian direction.

Many appear to find the task so difficult that they give it up. The former often feel they are working against the stream, even in the Church. Its preaching and teaching seems often to lead to an understanding of the Faith that leaves no room for linking faith and work. Is the industrial mission project unrealistic? Does it need to be changed? It is certainly right and helpful to raise these questions. Practitioners have a duty to heed the critique of the Church and continuously to rethink the grounds of their beliefs and re-evaluate goals and methods. If, at the end of the day, the project is demonstrably of value, then within the Church it deserves more support.

Abroad, missioners allege multinational companies, financial and capital manipulators, trade unions and other powerful institutions, cannot be addressed and will not change. They argue for change to begin where the poor and the powerless suffer, so that solidarity with the poorest must be the locus of the Church's mission. We in Scottish industrial mission are not unchallenged!

How Mission is perceived beyond Scotland

In a recent issue of the *Monthly Letter on Evangelism* of the World Council of Churches, Raymond Fung, the Evangelism Secretary, argued for a strategy for World Mission:

> ... *I propose that the churches, internationally and locally, make a permanent effort to be a credible sign to the vision described in Isaiah 65: 17-23. Here the prophet reported on God's preference for society. It is not paradise. There is death, and sweat, and toil. But in God's preference for the world, four elements are basic:*
>
> *Children do not die. Old people live full lives. Those who build houses live in them. Those who plant vineyards eat the fruit. I make the proposal as a first component part of a strategy for world mission because it is biblical, easy to understand, powerful in its appeal, capable of being worked out in action in different circumstances, and capable of rallying many churches whose unity is essential for world mission. I would like to see the churches proclaim in every neighbourhood that this four-point programme of Isaiah is what we stand for.*

Fung added that, alongside this effort, must go corporate worship and prayer, meaningful and available to all who work for the Isaiah vision. In our weakness, and 'shared woundedness', with prayer, Fung believes we can find the basis of solidarity between the Christianity and the world.

The German theologian, Jurgen Moltmann, has also written powerfully on mission. He speaks of Christianity as the community of those who, on the ground of the resurrection of Christ, wait for the Kingdom of God, and whose life is determined by this expectation. Consequently the Church's life and suffering, work and action in the world 'must be determined by the open foreland of its hopes for the world'.

The Church which follows Christ's mission to the world, serves the world. It is a Church of God where it is a Church for the world. But the Church serves humankind, not that the world may remain as it is, but to transform it.

Jim Wallis, the American evangelist, who came to Scotland in 1986, encouraged people to find personal faith in Jesus Christ by his own witness to the radical message of the Kingdom of God. Wallis has spent most of his adult life working amongst the poor for peace, community and racial integration. He spoke of how the vision of the Kingdom of God was being replaced by an American civic religion in which the Church's life had become wedded to generally accepted American values. A Church driven by its life in Jesus Christ will have very different values.

In Argentina, Jose Migues Bonnino believes that if people are to live by faith they cannot evade political struggle. In real encounter with the issues addressed by the political process, faith dies and is resurrected. It learns new ways of naming God and confessing Christ, of praying and receiving the Sacrament. In a community in Sao Paulo, a worker agreed: 'The Pope is right. Priests ought not to spend their time on "material things" like building churches and making collections. They should work at "spiritual things" like defending and helping the poor.' Bonnino complains that, 'Biblical and theological scholarship over the past fifty years has clearly established that dichotomies between the inner and the outward life, the spiritual and the material, the individual and the communal, theology and ethics, dichotomies on which much of theology, and particularly much of modern theology, has been built – are foreign to the basic outlook of biblical thought. Any theological ethics deserving of the name of biblical has to honour what we call the incarnational perspective'.

This is what Archbishop Temple meant when he said, fifty years ago, that Christianity claimed to be the 'most avowedly materialistic' of all religions.

Many of us in today's ministry and mission were influenced by the writings of Reinhold Niebuhr. His concern for human destiny in the context of modern culture, his discussion on the Kingdom of God and the struggle for justice, are still up to date. But in almost the final words of *Moral Man and Immoral Society*, he admits we are at least mercifully rid of some of our earlier illusions. In particular, we now know that 'we can no longer buy the highest satisfactions of the individual life at the expense of social injustice. We cannot build our individual ladders to heaven and leave the total human enterprise unredeemed of its excesses and corruptions'. He emphasised our need to be realistic.

It may also be an illusion that the collective life of mankind can achieve perfect justice, but in the struggle the agents of mission are in the right place.

Charles Birch, in the January 1985 *Ecumenical Review*, asked Christians to try to ' ... think synoptically about economics, politics, science, technology, industry, ethics and faith'. Drawing on this, Margaret Dewey, Editor of *Thinking Mission*, speaks of the unique contribution which the Christian Gospel can make if we can do so. She writes:

> *Economics and ecology are concerns to Christian mission because they have to do with God's creation and human responsibility. For Christians the 'ecology model that encompasses all life' is to be found in theology properly understood not as one academic subject among many, but as the Queen of Science which relates and gives meaning to all the others. Our faith, our Christian life, our mission, is not something private, but has to be concerned with the whole human condition, with what people do for a living and what they produce; how it is made, distributed, paid for and used; concerned not only with how individuals relate to each other but with how the groups and vested interests, and nations and races, relate to each other.*
>
> *Christians must therefore be equipped and supported to be part of the mission of Christ's Church and His Gospel at their own point of opportunity.*

Throughout the world, Christians are living side by side with neighbours who believe in other faiths. Christian mission has to remember that not all of God's truth is contained in Christianity. It may be comforting to some to proclaim that only when all the world becomes Christian will there be salvation and hope, but arrogant certainties are not a helpful platform for mission in a religiously plural world.

Dr Koyoma of Japan used the words 'painful vulnerability' to describe the reality of Christian life and action in today's missionary experience.

Some Missionary Practice elsewhere

After the Commission for World Mission and Evangelism had placed 'Resistance as a Form of Christian Witness' on its agenda in 1985, the World Council of Churches' Advisory Group on Urban-Rural Mission focused on it at its meeting in Recife in Brazil. Christians living under dictators began to understand resistance as not only a civic duty, but a Christian duty. 'For Christians, resistance is a key form of Christian witness and a fundamental act of faith.' Is this relevant in Britain? Are some of our political decisions hidden from the light of the Gospel? If we ignore the possibility, our mission will be flawed. It is a mistake to confine our Gospel and its proclamation to the pulpit, and to Christian prayer and study groups unrelated to events in the world, for God loves the world, and is in the world.

In July 1986, the Commission of World Mission and Evangelism of the WCC commended to the churches some reflections on urban rural mission in preparation for the 1989 World Mission conference. Industrialisation and urbanisation were concerns of the 1961 Third Assembly of the WCC and the programmes developed thereafter were assigned to the care of World Mission and Evangelism. Twenty-five years later, all this work of study and action has become an integral part of the movement called Urban Rural Mission (URM). URM is primarily 'a movement of men and women rooted in the Christian faith, who are called, along with others, to the mission of God to participate in the struggle of the exploited, marginalised and oppressed for justice and liberation'.

URM believes the Gospel teaches us that God, through Jesus Christ, exhorts the Church to side with the poor and the marginalised. It struggles to understand the causes of injustice. 'As an integral part of the total mission of the Church, URM is committed to continuing its deeper involvement in an ecumenism which transcends narrow denominational, or even religious affiliations, for the sake of fulfilling its vocation in the historical movement of people for justice and liberation – God's shalom.' It says the mission of God often begins with people in pain.

Politics must be taken seriously, as a vehicle for the transformation of the world into the Kingdom of God.

Industry can dominate the lives of people within it, and dramatically affect those who live in its shadow or who are sometimes pushed aside by its expansion. Some missioners have specialised in industrial mission, working with employees and managers. In urban areas people can experience poverty and deprivation at every level. So some have specialised in urban mission, working with communities, and voluntary organisations.

Yet others work with rural issues – including rural unemployment and poverty, lack of access to services, remoteness, and powerlessness. Each group of missionaries rightly feels that it is involved in part of the total mission of the Church. Occasionally some feel their particular work is the most strategic. Increasingly it is being recognised that industrial, urban and rural aspects of mission belong together. As one industrial missioner put it: 'For people in cities the industrial/urban and the rural are, in political, economic and personal terms, simply two sides of the same coin.'

Mission in the British Urban/Industrial Community

Some years ago, the William Temple Foundation published a stimulating document, *Involvement in Community*, which was commended to the churches when thinking of the way people are actually living. The simple plea to be 'in touch' or to seem relevant, was questioned. It suggested that much of the current use by the churches of community work as a vehicle of mission and service, would not meet the needs of people in major conurbations. It alleged the Church was not facing up to the structures, collectives and institutions which shape life; it was not facing up to what God was doing and saying in and through contemporary human experience.

One working rule of effective mission was found to be important. 'People to whom God matters must get in touch with that which matters to people.' If all talk of God has been confined to 'out of touch' cultic ghettos (the churches), there is no way of making sense of God until people to whom God matters can line up effectively with what matters to people. This means getting to where people are, usually well outside the churches, and staying with them long enough to have some chance of starting where they are. There God will be found and the Bible become a source of new life.

The Church of England Report, *Faith in the City,* provoked a similar reaction. Rejected by the Government, its main findings are directed at the Church.

The Church of Scotland General Assembly of 1986 committed the Church of Scotland to studying its implications. Many of Scotland's problems are similar, and caused by the name mixture of industrial and urban decay. It was entirely appropriate that this Report be given the closest attention, not only by those at the sharp end of urban problems in mission priority parishes, and by community and industrial missioners, but by congregations and church structures.

The Kairos document, *Challenge to the Church,* signed by over 150 Christian leaders in South Africa, at a time when apartheid was still in place, was a fundamental critique of state theology.

It was also severe in its criticism of 'church theology' which, it said, lacked social analysis. That theology 'tended to be an otherworldly affair that has very little, if anything, to do with the affairs of the world'. It is individualistic, and believes simplistically that God will intervene in his own good time, to right the wrongs of the world. It hardly needs saying that this way of thinking has no biblical foundation. *Challenge to the Church* argued for a prophetic theology and a transformation of church activities to serve the real needs of people and free the world. We should study this document again, not only for its insights into the South African situation, but as a tool of mission for our own work.

The Need for a New Missionary Approach in Scotland

These reflections on the nature of our Christian mission lead us to question how we undertake our own task in Scotland. Whilst it is clearly better for mission to specialise to be more effective, too wide a gap has opened up between parts of the same mission. We are therefore not building upon each other's work to make a more effective united witness. As soon as people commit themselves to Christ, we should be pointing them to the world as a sphere of missionary activity. For this they will need some understanding of the Bible and as they continue, some understanding of the way the world works. Trainers in Christian centres and in congregations need, therefore, to work more closely with urban and industrial missioners.

In-service courses for ministers should include further analysis and under-standing of the world of work to inform their preaching and give it some apparent connection with what happens for most people from Monday to Friday. Perhaps then more men will return to our congregations and both men and women will find worship and prayer mean more to them. In this regard, mission in the work place must be of assistance.

The Church of Scotland also has community ministers. How they relate to the wider Church is important. The main strength of work at community level is that it is locally rooted. At the same time, community ministers would benefit from links with each other. Local situations are often determined by wider political and social conditions. Protest groups and local organisations would be more effective if they combined to press for change in the wider structures.

The Church and its structures remain largely uninformed by the experiences of community ministers. Many urban concerns, unemployment, poverty, welfare and taxation, have, in the past, been addressed by industrial mission. Would it, therefore, not be wise to explore the possibility of greater co-operation between community ministry and industrial mission? Similarly, Boards of the General Assembly of the Church of Scotland, and also committees of presbyteries, must give careful attention to administrative matters, but they must find time to discuss issues arising from Scotland's changing society and the changing lives of its people.

At the Industry Year conference, convened by industrial mission and at which industrialists and trade unionists were present, a most effective biblical message was conveyed by our German colleague, Christa Springe.

She pointed to a woodcut she had hung on the wall. It portrayed a scene from the parable Jesus told of the man who fell among thieves and showed the Levite passing by on the other side. Having almost stepped over the victim, he passed purposefully by along a well delineated road. His path was sure, the road was clear, he did not stop to see the man lying there. But the picture was drawn from the perspective of the man set upon by a thief, lying on his back with his head on the ground. It was a bottom-up perspective. She challenged both the industrialists and the churches to try to see life from the point of view of the powerless and the poor, from the bottom up. Our mission will be more effective if this well-known parable is our constant study, from the perspective of the victim, and the basis of all our activity.

APPENDIX 1

Directors of the Society, Religion and Technology Project

DATE	NAME
6 May 1970 – September 1974	Dr John Francis
February 1975 – 31 January 1978	Dr Colin Pritchard
1 November 1978 – January 1983	Mr Iain O Macdonald
January 1983 – December 1985	Howard Davis
January 1986 – February 1992	Dr David J Pullinger
September 1992 –	Dr Donald Bruce

APPENDIX 2

Scottish Churches Industrial Mission Publications

FOR three periods, running over spans of four or five years at a time, regular monthly papers carrying news articles and comment for general distribution were produced. The first of these attempted a semi-tabloid style with a coloured title – *Worklife*. This ran for the first five years of the 1970s. There were bold headlines and pieces on, for example: 'Too much Overtime', 'Let's go for Quality', 'UCS Work in Perspective', 'A Voice from Europe', 'Who's afraid of Participation?', 'The Man in the Hot Seat', 'Is Growth still the Answer?' and 'Industry and the Community'.

Worklife normally had up to eight pages, with cartoons from Hamish Montgomery.

A later series, entitled *Newsletter for Christians in Industry*, with four pages in smaller type, ran for some fifty editions up to the 1980s. For a further five or six years, we published the *Newsletter of Scottish Churches Industrial Mission*, the intention being to speak less to the Christians in industry and more to the general industrial community.

Following the latter publication, a series of 'Blue Papers' was produced. They were largely written by different chaplains. They included:

'The Contribution of Liberation Theology to a Christian Response to Mass Unemployment' – by Erik Cramb.
'Response to Investment Policy' – by Hugh Ormiston.
'Along the Highway' – by John Prescott.
'Morality in a Market Economy' – by Donald M Ross.
'Some consequences of Industrial Change for Individuals and Families' – by Donald M Ross.
'The Papal Encyclical on Work' – by Frank Kennedy.
'A Window into Lay Consciousness and Lay Development in West Germany' – by Norman Orr.
'Scotland, a Struggle on the Periphery' – by Erik Cramb.
'Christ amid Cultural and Cosmic Crisis' – by Norman Orr.

Other titles were:

'A Christian at Work – four Studies for Congregational Groups'
'A Day in the Life of an Industrial Chaplain'
'A Supportive Church'
'A Working Concern'
'Being a Christian at Work'
'An Elder with a Different Remit'
'The Foreman – Forgotten Man'
'The Local Industrial Chaplain'
'The Social Charter – An Introduction'
'The Transforming Struggle'
'What is the Church doing in Industry?'
'What is Industrial Mission?'
'Work, Unemployment and Christian Faith'
'Lost Your Job?'
'Some Practical Responses for the Church in a Time of Unemployment'
'A Basic Manual for Industrial Chaplains'
'The Church and Daily Work'
'Psychological Effects of Redundancy'
'Shipbuilding Today and Tomorrow'

A very valuable series of Annual Reports from chaplains and their local committees was also produced. These included:

North East Scotland Industrial Mission Annual Report.
The Tayside Industrial Mission Annual Report.
The Forth Valley Industrial Mission Annual Report.

Major books were:

Christian Thinking about Industrial Life – by George Wilkie.
God's Working World – by Frank Kennedy.
Redundancy – a Personal Survival Kit.
The Role of Christians in the Trade Unions – by George Wilkie.
New Patterns of Work – edited by Hugh Ormiston and Donald M Ross.
A Woman's Place ... Women and Work – edited by Elizabeth Templeton.

APPENDIX 3

The Foreman — Forgotten Man

IF you are a foreman, you are one unit in an army 200,000 strong. But you have probably a more confused battleground than most other people in industry. It is maybe wrong to talk about a 'battleground'. For one thing, you are never quite sure who the enemy is. Is it time? Is it materials? Is it policy? Is it absenteeism? And maybe the battle you have fought and won a long time ago is still the daily experience of another foreman not half a mile away.

The foreman is a man with many pressures on him. *Worklife* magazine used to depict some of the turmoils of industry in the cartoon illustrations around the 'Wee Gaffer'. The 'Wee Gaffer' might have looked a bit like this:

APPENDIX 4

Index